A DRAFT OF
XXX CANTOS

BOOKS BY EZRA POUND

ABC of Reading. A primer in literary values. New Directions Paperbook 89

The Cantos of Ezra Pound. Cloth

The Classic Noh Theatre of Japan. Translations, with notes by Ernest Fenollosa and an essay on Noh by W. B. Yeats. NDP79

Collected Early Poems of Ezra Pound. Complete texts of Pound's first books of poems, 1908–1912. Edited by John Michael King, with an introduction by Louis L. Martz. NDP540

Confucius. Translations of Chinese classics. NDP285

Confucius to Cummings. An anthology of poetry from many languages. Edited, with notes, by Pound and Marcella Spann. Cloth & NDP126

A Draft of XXX Cantos. NDP690

Elektra. Translation, with Rudd Fleming, of Sophokles' tragedy. NDP683

Ezra Pound and Dorothy Shakespear: Their Letters 1909–1914. Edited by Omar S. Pound and A. Walton Litz. Cloth

Ezra Pound and Music: The Complete Criticism. Edited by R. Murray Schafer. Cloth

Ezra Pound and the Visual Arts. Edited by Harriet Zinnes. Cloth

Gaudier-Brzeska. A memoir. NDP372

Guide to Kulchur. A study of aspects of world culture. NDP257

Literary Essays of Ezra Pound. Edited, with an introduction, by T. S. Eliot. NDP250

Love Poems of Ancient Egypt. Translations by Pound and Noel Stock. NDP178

Pavannes and Divigations. Lighter prose and poetry. NDP397

Personae. Definitive collected shorter poems. Revised edition, prepared by Lea Baechler and A. Walton Litz. Cloth

Pound/Ford: The Story of a Literary Friendship. Edited with an introduction and narrative commentary by Brita Lindberg-Seyersted. Cloth

Pound/Joyce: Letters and Essays. Edited by Forrest Read. NDP296

Pound/Lewis: The Letters of Ezra Pound and Wyndham Lewis. Edited, with an introduction, by Timothy Materer. Cloth

Pound/Zukofsky. Selected Letters of Ezra Pound and Louis Zukofsky. Edited by Barry Ahearn. Cloth

Selected Cantos. Pound's own selection. NDP304

Selected Letters 1907–1941. Edited, with an introduction, by D. D. Paige. NDP317

Selected Poems. NDP66

Selected Prose 1909–1965. Edited, with an introduction, by William Cookson. NDP396

The Spirit of Romance. A survey of Romance literature. NDP266

Translations. Pound's translations of poetry from many languages. Introduction by Hugh Kenner. NDP145

Women of Trachis. Translation of Sophokles' *Trachiniae.* NDP597

A DRAFT OF

XXX

CANTOS

BY EZRA POUND

A NEW DIRECTIONS BOOK

Manufactured in the United States of America
New Directions Books are published on acid-free paper.
First published as New Directions Paperbook 690 in 1990
Originally published clothbound by Farrar & Rhinehart (1933); re-
issued by New Directions (1940)
Published simultaneously in Canada by Penguin Books Canada
Limited

Library of Congress Cataloging in Publication Data
Pound, Ezra, 1885-1972.
    [Cantos.   Canto 1-30]
    A draft of XXX cantos / by Ezra Pound.
        p.   cm.—(New Directions paperbook; 690)
    ISBN 0-8112-1128-2 (alk. paper)
    I. Title.   II.   Title: Draft of thirty cantos.
PS3531.082C29   1990
811'.52—dc20   89-13432
                                                  CIP

New Directions Books are published for James Laughlin
by New Directions Publishing Corporation,
80 Eighth Avenue, New York 10011

A DRAFT OF
X X X   C A N T O S

I

AND then went down to the ship,
Set keel to breakers, forth on the godly sea, and
We set up mast and sail on that swart ship,
Bore sheep aboard her, and our bodies also
Heavy with weeping, and winds from sternward
Bore us out onward with bellying canvas,
Circe's this craft, the trim-coifed goddess.
Then sat we amidships, wind jamming the tiller,
Thus with stretched sail, we went over sea till day's end.
Sun to his slumber, shadows o'er all the ocean,
Came we then to the bounds of deepest water,
To the Kimmerian lands, and peopled cities
Covered with close-webbed mist, unpierced ever
With glitter of sun-rays
Nor with stars stretched, nor looking back from heaven
Swartest night stretched over wretched men there.
The ocean flowing backward, came we then to the place
Aforesaid by Circe.
Here did they rites, Perimedes and Eurylochus,
And drawing sword from my hip
I dug the ell-square pitkin;
Poured we libations unto each the dead,
First mead and then sweet wine, water mixed with white flour.
Then prayed I many a prayer to the sickly death's-heads;
As set in Ithaca, sterile bulls of the best
For sacrifice, heaping the pyre with goods,
A sheep to Tiresias only, black and a bell-sheep.
Dark blood flowed in the fosse,
Souls out of Erebus, cadaverous dead, of brides
Of youths and of the old who had borne much;
Souls stained with recent tears, girls tender,

Men many, mauled with bronze lance heads,
Battle spoil, bearing yet dreory arms,
These many crowded about me; with shouting,
Pallor upon me, cried to my men for more beasts;
Slaughtered the herds, sheep slain of bronze;
Poured ointment, cried to the gods,
To Pluto the strong, and praised Proserpine;
Unsheathed the narrow sword,
I sat to keep off the impetuous impotent dead,
Till I should hear Tiresias.
But first Elpenor came, our friend Elpenor,
Unburied, cast on the wide earth,
Limbs that we left in the house of Circe,
Unwept, unwrapped in sepulchre, since toils urged other.
Pitiful spirit.   And I cried in hurried speech:
" Elpenor, how art thou come to this dark coast?
" Cam'st thou afoot, outstripping seamen? "
                    And he in heavy speech:
" Ill fate and abundant wine.   I slept in Circe's ingle.
" Going down the long ladder unguarded,
" I fell against the buttress,
" Shattered the nape-nerve, the soul sought Avernus.
" But thou, O King, I bid remember me, unwept, unburied,
" Heap up mine arms, be tomb by sea-bord, and inscribed:
" *A man of no fortune, and with a name to come.*
" And set my oar up, that I swung mid fellows."

And Anticlea came, whom I beat off, and then Tiresias Theban,
Holding his golden wand, knew me, and spoke first:
" A second time? why? man of ill star,
" Facing the sunless dead and this joyless region?
" Stand from the fosse, leave me my bloody bever
" For soothsay. "
                    And I stepped back,
And he strong with the blood, said then: " Odysseus

" Shalt return through spiteful Neptune, over dark seas,
" Lose all companions. "   And then Anticlea came.
Lie quiet Divus.   I mean, that is Andreas Divus,
In officina Wecheli, 1538, out of Homer.
And he sailed, by Sirens and thence outward and away
And unto Circe.

      Venerandam,
In the Cretan's phrase, with the golden crown, Aphrodite,
Cypri munimenta sortita est, mirthful, oricalchi, with golden
Girdles and breast bands, thou with dark eyelids
Bearing the golden bough of Argicida.   So that:

II

Hang it all, Robert Browning,
    there can be but the one "Sordello."
    But Sordello, and my Sordello?
    Lo Sordels si fo di Mantovana.
So-shu churned in the sea.
Seal sports in the spray-whited circles of cliff-wash,
Sleek head, daughter of Lir,
        eyes of Picasso
Under black fur-hood, lithe daughter of Ocean;
And the wave runs in the beach-groove:
"Eleanor, ἐλέναυς and ἐλέπτολις!"
        And poor old Homer blind, blind, as a bat,
Ear, ear for the sea-surge, murmur of old men's voices:
"Let her go back to the ships,
Back among Grecian faces, lest evil come on our own,
Evil and further evil, and a curse cursed on our children,
Moves, yes she moves like a goddess
And has the face of a god
        and the voice of Schoeney's daughters,
And doom goes with her in walking,
Let her go back to the ships,
        back among Grecian voices."
And by the beach-run, Tyro,
        Twisted arms of the sea-god,
Lithe sinews of water, gripping her, cross-hold,
And the blue-gray glass of the wave tents them,
Glare azure of water, cold-welter, close cover.
Quiet sun-tawny sand-stretch,
The gulls broad out their wings,
        nipping between the splay feathers;

Snipe come for their bath,
              bend out their wing-joints,
Spread wet wings to the sun-film,
And by Scios,
              to left of the Naxos passage,
Naviform rock overgrown,
              algæ cling to its edge,
There is a wine-red glow in the shallows,
              a tin flash in the sun-dazzle.

The ship landed in Scios,
              men wanting spring-water,
And by the rock-pool a young boy loggy with vine-must,
              " To Naxos? Yes, we'll take you to Naxos,
Cum' along lad. " " Not that way! "
" Aye, that way is Naxos."
              And I said: " It's a straight ship."
And an ex-convict out of Italy
              knocked me into the fore-stays,
(He was wanted for manslaughter in Tuscany)
              And the whole twenty against me,
Mad for a little slave money.
              And they took her out of Scios
And off her course...
              And the boy came to, again, with the racket,
And looked out over the bows,
              and to eastward, and to the Naxos passage.
God-sleight then, god-sleight:
              Ship stock fast in sea-swirl,
Ivy upon the oars, King Pentheus,
              grapes with no seed but sea-foam,
Ivy in scupper-hole.
Aye, I, Acœtes, stood there,
              and the god stood by me,
Water cutting under the keel,

7

Sea-break from stern forrards,
        wake running off from the bow,
And where was gunwale, there now was vine-trunk,
And tenthril where cordage had been,
        grape-leaves on the rowlocks,
Heavy vine on the oarshafts,
And, out of nothing, a breathing,
        hot breath on my ankles,
Beasts like shadows in glass,
        a furred tail upon nothingness.
Lynx-purr, and heathery smell of beasts,
        where tar smell had been,
Sniff and pad-foot of beasts,
        eye-glitter out of black air.
The sky overshot, dry, with no tempest,
Sniff and pad-foot of beasts,
        fur brushing my knee-skin,
Rustle of airy sheaths,
        dry forms in the *æther*.
And the ship like a keel in ship-yard,
        slung like an ox in smith's sling,
Ribs stuck fast in the ways,
        grape-cluster over pin-rack,
        void air taking pelt.
Lifeless air become sinewed,
        feline leisure of panthers,
Leopards sniffing the grape shoots by scupper-hole,
Crouched panthers by fore-hatch,
And the sea blue-deep about us,
        green-ruddy in shadows,
And Lyæus: " From now, Acœtes, my altars,
Fearing no bondage,
        fearing no cat of the wood,
Safe with my lynxes,
        feeding grapes to my leopards,

Olibanum is my incense,
        the vines grow in my homage."

The back-swell now smooth in the rudder-chains,
Black snout of a porpoise
        where Lycabs had been,
Fish-scales on the oarsmen.
        And I worship.
I have seen what I have seen.
        When they brought the boy I said:
" He has a god in him,
        though I do not know which god."
And they kicked me into the fore-stays.
I have seen what I have seen:
        Medon's face like the face of a dory,
Arms shrunk into fins.   And you, Pentheus,
Had as well listen to Tiresias, and to Cadmus,
        or your luck will go out of you.
Fish-scales over groin muscles,
        lynx-purr amid sea...
And of a later year,
        pale in the wine-red algæ,
If you will lean over the rock,
        the coral face under wave-tinge,
Rose-paleness under water-shift,
        Ileuthyeria, fair Dafne of sea-bords,
The swimmer's arms turned to branches,
Who will say in what year,
        fleeing what band of tritons,
The smooth brows, seen, and half seen,
        now ivory stillness.

And So-shu churned in the sea, So-shu also,
        using the long moon for a churn-stick...
Lithe turning of water,
        sinews of Poseidon,

Black azure and hyaline,
        glass wave over Tyro,
Close cover, unstillness,
        bright welter of wave-cords,
Then quiet water,
        quiet in the buff sands,
Sea-fowl stretching wing-joints,
        splashing in rock-hollows and sand-hollows
In the wave-runs by the half-dune;
Glass-glint of wave in the tide-rips against sunlight,
        pallor of Hesperus,
Grey peak of the wave,
        wave, colour of grape's pulp,

Olive grey in the near,
        far, smoke grey of the rock-slide,
Salmon-pink wings of the fish-hawk
        cast grey shadows in water,
The tower like a one-eyed great goose
        cranes up out of the olive-grove,

And we have heard the fauns chiding Proteus
        in the smell of hay under the olive-trees,
And the frogs singing against the fauns
        in the half-light.
And...

III

I SAT on the Dogana's steps
 For the gondolas cost too much, that year,
 And there were not " those girls ", there was one face,
 And the Buccentoro twenty yards off, howling " Stretti ",
And the lit cross-beams, that year, in the Morosini,
And peacocks in Koré's house, or there may have been.
       Gods float in the azure air,
Bright gods and Tuscan, back before dew was shed.
Light: and the first light, before ever dew was fallen.
Panisks, and from the oak, dryas,
And from the apple, mælid,
Through all the wood, and the leaves are full of voices,
A-whisper, and the clouds bowe over the lake,
And there are gods upon them,
And in the water, the almond-white swimmers,
The silvery water glazes the upturned nipple,
       As Poggio has remarked.
Green veins in the turquoise,
Or, the gray steps lead up under the cedars.

My Cid rode up to Burgos,
Up to the studded gate between two towers,
Beat with his lance butt, and the child came out,
Una niña de nueve años,
To the little gallery over the gate, between the towers,
Reading the writ, voce tinnula:
That no man speak to, feed, help Ruy Diaz,
On pain to have his heart out, set on a pike spike
And both his eyes torn out, and all his goods sequestered,
" And here, Myo Cid, are the seals,
The big seal and the writing."
And he came down from Bivar, Myo Cid,

With no hawks left there on their perches,
And no clothes there in the presses,
And left his trunk with Raquel and Vidas,
That big box of sand, with the pawn-brokers,
To get pay for his menie;
Breaking his way to Valencia.
Ignez da Castro murdered, and a wall
Here stripped, here made to stand.
Drear waste, the pigment flakes from the stone,
Or plaster flakes, Mantegna painted the wall.
Silk tatters, " Nec Spe Nec Metu."

IV

PALACE in smoky light,
Troy but a heap of smouldering boundary stones,
ANAXIFORMINGES!   Aurunculeia!
Hear me.   Cadmus of Golden Prows!
The silver mirrors catch the bright stones and flare,
Dawn, to our waking, drifts in the green cool light;
Dew-haze blurs, in the grass, pale ankles moving.
Beat, beat, whirr, thud, in the soft turf
            under the apple trees,
Choros nympharum, goat-foot, with the pale foot alternate;
Crescent of blue-shot waters, green-gold in the shallows,
A black cock crows in the sea-foam;

And by the curved, carved foot of the couch,
            claw-foot and lion head, an old man seated
Speaking in the low drone... :
                Ityn!
Et ter flebiliter, Ityn, Ityn!
And she went toward the window and cast her down,
        " All the while, the while, swallows crying:
Ityn!
        " It is Cabestan's heart in the dish."
        " It is Cabestan's heart in the dish?
        " No other taste shall change this."
And she went toward the window,
            the slim white stone bar
Making a double arch;
Firm even fingers held to the firm pale stone;
Swung for a moment,
            and the wind out of Rhodez
Caught in the full of her sleeve.
        . . . the swallows crying:

'Tis. 'Tis. Ytis!
      Actæon...
           and a valley,
The valley is thick with leaves, with leaves, the trees,
The sunlight glitters, glitters a-top,
Like a fish-scale roof,
           Like the church roof in Poictiers
If it were gold.
           Beneath it, beneath it
Not a ray, not a slivver, not a spare disc of sunlight
Flaking the black, soft water;
Bathing the body of nymphs, of nymphs, and Diana,
Nymphs, white-gathered about her, and the air, air,
Shaking, air alight with the goddess,
           fanning their hair in the dark,
Lifting, lifting and waffing:
Ivory dipping in silver,
           Shadow'd, o'ershadow'd
Ivory dipping in silver,
Not a splotch, not a lost shatter of sunlight.
Then Actæon: Vidal,
Vidal. It is old Vidal speaking,
           stumbling along in the wood,
Not a patch, not a lost shimmer of sunlight,
           the pale hair of the goddess.

The dogs leap on Actæon,
      " Hither, hither, Actæon,"
Spotted stag of the wood;
Gold, gold, a sheaf of hair,
           Thick like a wheat swath,
Blaze, blaze in the sun,
           The dogs leap on Actæon.

Stumbling, stumbling along in the wood,
Muttering, muttering Ovid:
      " Pergusa... pool... pool... Gargaphia,
" Pool... pool of Salmacis."
        The empty armour shakes as the cygnet moves.

Thus the light rains, thus pours, *e lo soleils plovil*
The liquid and rushing crystal
      beneath the knees of the gods.
Ply over ply, thin glitter of water;
Brook film bearing white petals.
The pines at Takasago
      grow with the pines of Isé!
The water whirls up the bright pale sand in the spring's mouth
" Behold the Tree of the Visages! "
Forked branch-tips, flaming as if with lotus.
      Ply over ply
The shallow eddying fluid,
      beneath the knees of the gods.

Torches melt in the glare
      set flame of the corner cook-stall,
Blue agate casing the sky (as at Gourdon that time)
      the sputter of resin,
Saffron sandal so petals the narrow foot: Hymenæus Io!
      Hymen, Io Hymenæe!   Aurunculeia!
A scarlet flower is cast on the blanch-white stone.

      And Sō-Gyoku, saying:
" This wind, sire, is the king's wind,
      This wind is wind of the palace,
Shaking imperial water-jets."
      And Ran-ti, opening his collar:
" This wind roars in the earth's bag,
      it lays the water with rushes;

No wind is the king's wind.
> Let every cow keep her calf."
" This wind is held in gauze curtains..."
> " No wind is the king's..."

The camel drivers sit in the turn of the stairs,
> Look down on Ecbatan of plotted streets,
" Danaë!   Danaë!
> What wind is the king's? "
Smoke hangs on the stream,
The peach-trees shed bright leaves in the water,
Sound drifts in the evening haze,
> The bark scrapes at the ford,
Gilt rafters above black water,
> Three steps in an open field,
Gray stone-posts leading...

Père Henri Jacques would speak with the Sennin, on Rokku,
Mount Rokku between the rock and the cedars,
Polhonac,
As Gyges on Thracian platter set the feast,
Cabestan, Tereus,
> It is Cabestan's heart in the dish,
Vidal, or Ecbatan, upon the gilded tower in Ecbatan
Lay the god's bride, lay ever, waiting the golden rain.
By Garonne.   " Saave! "
The Garonne is thick like paint,
Procession, — " Et sa'ave, sa'ave, sa'ave Regina! " —
Moves like a worm, in the crowd.
Adige, thin film of images,
Across the Adige, by Stefano, Madonna in hortulo,
As Cavalcanti had seen her.
> The Centaur's heel plants in the earth loam.
And we sit here...
> there in the arena...

V

GREAT bulk, huge mass, thesaurus;
  Ecbatan, the clock ticks and fades out
  The bride awaiting the god's touch; Ecbatan,
  City of patterned streets; again the vision:
Down in the viæ stradæ, toga'd the crowd, and arm'd,
Rushing on populous business,
and from parapet looked down
and North was Egypt,
  the celestial Nile, blue deep,
  cutting low barren land,
Old men and camels
    working the water-wheels;
Measureless seas and stars,
Iamblichus' light,
  the souls ascending,
Sparks like a partridge covey,
  Like the " ciocco ", brand struck in the game.
" Et omniformis ": Air, fire, the pale soft light.
Topaz I manage, and three sorts of blue;
  but on the barb of time.
The fire? always, and the vision always,
Ear dull, perhaps, with the vision, flitting
And fading at will. Weaving with points of gold,
Gold-yellow, saffron... The roman shoe, Aurunculeia's
And come shuffling feet, and cries " Da nuces!
" Nuces! " praise, and Hymenæus " brings the girl to her man "
Or " here Sextus had seen her."
Titter of sound about me, always.
  and from " Hesperus..."
Hush of the older song: " Fades light from sea-crest,
" And in Lydia walks with pair'd women
" Peerless among the pairs, that once in Sardis

17

" In satieties...

    Fades the light from the sea, and many things
" Are set abroad and brought to mind of thee,"
And the vinestocks lie untended, new leaves come to the shoots,
North wind nips on the bough, and seas in heart
Toss up chill crests,

    And the vine stocks lie untended
And many things are set abroad and brought to mind
Of thee, Atthis, unfruitful.

    The talks ran long in the night.
And from Mauleon, fresh with a new earned grade,
In maze of approaching rain-steps, Poicebot—
The air was full of women,

    And Savairic Mauleon
Gave him his land and knight's fee, and he wed the woman.
Came lust of travel on him, of *romerya*;
And out of England a knight with slow-lifting eyelids
Lei fassa furar a del, put glamour upon her...
And left her an eight months gone.

    " Came lust of woman upon him,"
Poicebot, now on North road from Spain
(Sea-change, a grey in the water)

    And in small house by town's edge
Found a woman, changed and familiar face;
Hard night, and parting at morning.

And Pieire won the singing, Pieire de Maensac,
Song or land on the throw, and was *dreitz hom*
And had De Tierci's wife and with the war they made:

    Troy in Auvergnat
While Menelaus piled up the church at port
He kept Tyndarida. Dauphin stood with de Maensac.

John Borgia is bathed at last. (Clock-tick pierces the vision)
Tiber, dark with the cloak, wet cat gleaming in patches.

Click of the hooves, through garbage,
Clutching the greasy stone. " And the cloak floated."
Slander is up betimes.

       But Varchi of Florence,
Steeped in a different year, and pondering Brutus,
Then " Σίγα μαλ' αὖθις δευτέραν!
" Dog-eye!! " (to Alessandro)
        " Whether for love of Florence," Varchi leaves it,
Saying " I saw the man, came up with him at Venice,
" I, one wanting the facts,
" And no mean labour... Or for a privy spite? "
Our Benedetto leaves it,
But: " I saw the man. *Se pia?*
" O empia? For Lorenzaccio had thought of stroke in the open
But uncertain (for the Duke went never unguarded)
" And would have thrown him from wall
" Yet feared this might not end him," or lest Alessandro
Know not by whom death came, O se credesse
" If when the foot slipped, when death came upon him,
" Lest cousin Duke Alessandro think he had fallen alone,
" No friend to aid him in falling."
                    Caina attende.
The lake of ice there below me.
And all of this, runs Varchi, dreamed out beforehand
In Perugia, caught in the star-maze by Del Carmine,
Cast on a natal paper, set with an exegesis, told,
All told to Alessandro, told thrice over,
Who held his death for a doom.
In abuleia. But Don Lorenzino
Whether for love of Florence ... but
" O se morisse, credesse caduto da sè "
Σίγα, σίγα
Schiavoni, caught on the wood-barge,
Gives out the afterbirth, Giovanni Borgia,
Trails out no more at nights, where Barabello

Prods the Pope's elephant, and gets no crown, where Mozarello
Takes the Calabrian roadway, and for ending
Is smothered beneath a mule,
                a poet's ending,
Down a stale well-hole, oh a poet's ending. " Sanazarro
" Alone out of all the court was faithful to him "
For the gossip of Naples' trouble drifts to North,
Fracastor (lightning was midwife) Cotta, and Ser D'Alviano,
Al poco giorno ed al gran cerchio d'ombra,
Talk the talks out with Navighero,
Burner of yearly Martials,
                (The slavelet is mourned in vain)
And the next comer says " Were nine wounds,
" Four men, white horse.   Held on the saddle before him..."
Hooves clink and slick on the cobbles.
Schiavoni... cloak... " Sink the damn thing! "
Splash wakes that chap on the wood-barge.
Tiber catching the nap, the moonlit velvet,
A wet cat gleaming in patches.
                " Se pia," Varchi,
" O empia, ma risoluto
" E terribile deliberazione."
                Both sayings run in the wind,
Ma se morisse!

WHAT you have done, Odysseus,
  We know what you have done...
And that Guillaume sold out his ground rents
(Seventh of Poitiers, Ninth of Aquitain).
 " Tant las fotei com auzirets
 " Cen e quatre vingt et veit vetz..."
The stone is alive in my hand, the crops
  will be thick in my death-year...
Till Louis is wed with Eleanor
And had (He, Guillaume) a son that had to wife
The Duchess of Normandia whose daughter
Was wife to King Henry e maire del rei jove...
Went over sea till day's end (he, Louis, with Eleanor)
Coming at last to Acre.
" Ongla, oncle " saith Arnaut
  Her uncle commanded in Acre,
That had known her in girlhood
  (Theseus, son of Aegeus)
And he, Louis, was not at ease in that town,
And was not at ease by Jordan
As she rode out to the palm-grove
Her scarf in Saladin's cimier.
Divorced her in that year, he Louis,
  divorcing thus Aquitaine.
And that year Plantagenet married her
  (that had dodged past 17 suitors)
Et quand lo reis Lois lo entendit
  mout er fasché.
Nauphal, Vexis, Harry joven
In pledge for all his life and life of all his heirs
Shall have Gisors, and Vexis, Neufchastel
But if no issue Gisors shall revert...

" Need not wed Alix... in the name
Trinity holy indivisible... Richard our brother
Need not wed Alix once his father's ward and...
But whomso he choose...for Alix, etc...

Eleanor, domna jauzionda, mother of Richard,
Turning on thirty years (wd. have been years before this)
By river-marsh, by galleried church-porch,
Malemorte, Correze, to whom:
      " My Lady of Ventadour
" Is shut by Eblis in
" And will not hawk nor hunt
      nor get her free in the air
" Nor watch fish rise to bait
" Nor the glare-wing'd flies alight in the creek's edge
" Save in my absence, Madame.
      ' Que la lauzeta mover '
" Send word I ask you to Eblis
      you have seen that maker
" And finder of songs so far afield as this
" That he may free her,
      who sheds such light in the air."

E lo Sordels si fo di Mantovana,
Son of a poor knight, Sier Escort,
And he delighted himself in chançons
And mixed with the men of the court
And went to the court of Richard Saint Boniface
And was there taken with love for his wife
      Cunizza, da Romano,
That freed her slaves on a Wednesday
Masnatas et servos, witness
Picus de Farinatis
and Don Elinus and Don Lipus
      sons of Farinato de' Farinati

" free of person, free of will
" free to buy, witness, sell, testate."
A marito subtraxit ipsam...
      dictum Sordellum concubuisse:
       " Winter and Summer I sing of her grace,
       As the rose is fair, so fair is her face,
       Both Summer and Winter I sing of her,
       The snow makyth me to remember her."

And Cairels was of Sarlat...
                Theseus from Troezene
And they wd. have given him poison
But for the shape of his sword-hilt.

VII

ELEANOR (she spoiled in a British climate)
    Ἔλανδρος and Ἑλέπτολις, and
        poor old Homer blind,
        blind as a bat,
Ear, ear for the sea-surge;
        rattle of old men's voices.
And then the phantom Rome,
        marble narrow for seats
" Si pulvis nullus " said Ovid,
" Erit, nullum tamen excute."
Then file and candles, e li mestiers ecoutes;
Scene for the battle only, but still scene,
Pennons and standards y cavals armatz
Not mere succession of strokes, sightless narration,
And Dante's " ciocco," brand struck in the game.

Un peu moisi, plancher plus bas que le jardin.

" Contre le lambris, fauteuil de paille,
" Un vieux piano, et sous le baromètre..."

The old men's voices, beneath the columns of false marble,
The modish and darkish walls,
Discreeter gilding, and the panelled wood
Suggested, for the leasehold is
Touched with an imprecision... about three squares;
The house too thick, the paintings
a shade too oiled.
And the great domed head, *con gli occhi onesti e tardi*
Moves before me, phantom with weighted motion,
Grave incessu, drinking the tone of things,
And the old voice lifts itself
        weaving an endless sentence.

We also made ghostly visits, and the stair
That knew us, found us again on the turn of it,
Knocking at empty rooms, seeking for buried beauty;
And the sun-tanned, gracious and well-formed fingers
Lift no latch of bent bronze, no Empire handle
Twists for the knocker's fall; no voice to answer.
A strange concierge, in place of the gouty-footed.
Sceptic against all this one seeks the living,
Stubborn against the fact. The wilted flowers
Brushed out a seven year since, of no effect.
Damn the partition! Paper, dark brown and stretched,
Flimsy and damned partition.
              Ione, dead the long year
My lintel, and Liu Ch'e's lintel.
Time blacked out with the rubber.
              The Elysée carries a name on
And the bus behind me gives me a date for peg;
Low ceiling and the Erard and the silver,
These are in " time." Four chairs, the bow-front dresser,
The panier of the desk, cloth top sunk in.
              " Beer-bottle on the statue's pediment!
" That, Fritz, is the era, to-day against the past,
" Contemporary." And the passion endures.
Against their action, aromas. Rooms, against chronicles.
Smaragdos, chrysolithos; De Gama wore striped pants in Africa
And " Mountains of the sea gave birth to troops ";

Le vieux commode en acajou:
              beer-bottles of various strata,
But *is* she dead as Tyro? In seven years?
   Ελέναυς, ἕλανδρος, ἐλέπτολις
The sea runs in the beach-groove, shaking the floated pebbles,
Eleanor!
              The scarlet curtain throws a less scarlet shadow;

25

Lamplight at Buovilla, e quel remir,
                And all that day
Nicea moved before me
And the cold grey air troubled her not
For all her naked beauty, bit not the tropic skin,
And the long slender feet lit on the curb's marge
And her moving height went before me,
                We alone having being.
And all that day, another day:
                Thin husks I had known as men,
Dry casques of departed locusts
                speaking a shell of speech...
Propped between chairs and table...
Words like the locust-shells, moved by no inner being;
                A dryness calling for death;

Another day, between walls of a sham Mycenian,
" Toc " sphinxes, sham-Memphis columns,
And beneath the jazz a cortex, a stiffness or stillness,
                Shell of the older house.
Brown-yellow wood, and the no colour plaster,
Dry professorial talk...
                now stilling the ill beat music,
House expulsed by this house.

                Square even shoulders and the satin skin,
Gone cheeks of the dancing woman,
                Still the old dead dry talk, gassed out —
It is ten years gone, makes stiff about her a glass,
A petrefaction of air.
                The old room of the tawdry class asserts itself;
The young men, never!
                Only the husk of talk.
O voi che siete in piccioletta barca,
Dido choked up with sobs, for her Sicheus

Lies heavy in my arms, dead weight
       Drowning, with tears, new Eros,

And the life goes on, mooning upon bare hills;
Flame leaps from the hand, the rain is listless,
Yet drinks the thirst from our lips,
       solid as echo,
Passion to breed a form in shimmer of rain-blur;
But Eros drowned, drowned, heavy-half dead with tears
       For dead Sicheus.

Life to make mock of motion:
For the husks, before me, move,
       The words rattle: shells given out by shells.
The live man, out of lands and prisons,
       shakes the dry pods,
Probes for old wills and friendships, and the big locust-casques
Bend to the tawdry table,
Lift up their spoons to mouths, put forks in cutlets,
And make sound like the sound of voices.
       Lorenzaccio
Being more live than they, more full of flames and voices.
Ma se morisse!
       Credesse caduto da sè, ma se morisse.
And the tall indifference moves,
       a more living shell,
Drift in the air of fate, dry phantom, but intact.
O Alessandro, chief and thrice warned, watcher,
       Eternal watcher of things,
Of things, of men, of passions.
       Eyes floating in dry, dark air,
E biondo, with glass-grey iris, with an even side-fall of hair
The stiff, still features.

VIII

THESE fragments you have shelved (shored).
      " Slut! " " Bitch! " Truth and Calliope
      Slanging each other sous les lauriers:
      That Alessandro was negroid.   And Malatesta
Sigismund:
            Frater tamquam
Et compater carissime: tergo
                        ...hanni de
                        ..dicis
                        ...entia
Equivalent to:
                        Giohanni of the Medici,
                        Florence.
Letter received, and in the matter of our Messire Gianozio,
One from him also, sent on in form and with all due dispatch,
Having added your wishes and memoranda.
As to arranging peace between you and the King of Ragona,
So far as I am concerned, it wd.
Give me the greatest possible pleasure,
At any rate nothing wd. give me more pleasure
      or be more acceptable to me,
And I shd. like to be party to it, as was promised me,
            either as participant or adherent.
As for my service money,
Perhaps you and your father wd. draw it
And send it on to me as quickly as possible.
And tell the *Maestro di pentore*
That there can be no question of
His painting the walls for the moment,
As the mortar is not yet dry
And it wd. be merely work chucked away
                  (*buttato via*)

But I want it to be quite clear, that until the chapels are ready
I will arrange for him to paint something else
So that both he and I shall
Get as much enjoyment as possible from it,
And in order that he may enter my service
And also because you write me that he needs cash,
I want to arrange with him to give him so much per year
And to assure him that he will get the sum agreed on.
You may say that I will deposit security
For him wherever he likes.
And let me have a clear answer,
For I mean to give him good treatment
So that he may come to live the rest
Of his life in my lands —
Unless you put him off it —
And for this I mean to make due provision,
So that he can work as he likes,
Or waste his time as he likes
(*affatigandose per suo piacere o no
non gli manchera la provixione mai*)

never lacking provision.

SIGISMUNDUS PANDOLPHUS DE MALATESTIS
*In campo Illus. Domini Venetorum die 7
aprilis* 1449 *contra Cremonam*

    . . . . . and because the aforesaid most illustrious
Duke of Milan
Is content and wills that the aforesaid Lord Sigismundo
Go into the service of the most magnificent commune
of the Florentines
For alliance defensive of the two states,
Therefore between the aforesaid Illustrious Sigismund
And the respectable man Agnolo della Stufa,
                    ambassador, sindic and procurator
Appointed by the ten of the baily, etc., the half

Of these 50,000 florins, free of attainder,
For 1400 cavalry and four hundred foot
To come into the terrene of the commune
                    or elsewhere in Tuscany
As please the ten of the Baily,
And to be himself there with them in the service
of the commune
With his horsemen and his footmen
                    (*gente di cavallo e da pie*) etc.
                    Aug. 5 1452, *register of the Ten of the Baily.*

From the forked rocks of Penna and Billi, on Carpegna
with the road leading under the cliff,
                    in the wind-shelter into Tuscany,
And the north road, toward the Marecchia
                    the mud-stretch full of cobbles.

Lyra:
" Ye spirits who of olde were in this land
Each under Love, and shaken,
Go with your lutes, awaken
The summer within her mind,
Who hath not Helen for peer
                    Yseut nor Batsabe."
With the interruption:
                    Magnifico, compater et carissime
                    (Johanni di Cosimo)
Venice has taken me on again
                    At 7,000 a month, *fiorini di Camera.*
For 2,000 horse and four hundred footmen,
And it rains here by the gallon,
We have had to dig a new ditch.
In three or four days
I shall try to set up the bombards.

Under the plumes, with the flakes and small wads of colour
Showering from the balconies

30

With the sheets spread from windows,
             with leaves and small branches pinned on them,
Arras hung from the railings; out of the dust,
With pheasant tails upright on their forelocks,
             The small white horses, the
Twelve girls riding in order, green satin in pannier'd habits;
Under the baldachino, silver'd with heavy stitches,
Bianca Visconti, with Sforza,
The peasant's son and the duchess,
To Rimini, and to the wars southward,
Boats drawn on the sand, red-orange sails in the creek's mouth,
For two days' pleasure, mostly *" la pesca,"* fishing,
Di cui in the which he, Francesco, *godeva molto.*
             To the war southward
In which he, at that time, received an excellent hiding.
And the Greek emperor was in Florence
             (Ferrara having the pest)
And with him Gemisthus Plethon
Talking of the war about the temple at Delphos,
And of POSEIDON, *concret Allgemeine,*
And telling of how Plato went to Dionysius of Syracuse
Because he had observed that tyrants
Were most efficient in all that they set their hands to,
But he was unable to persuade Dionysius
To any amelioration.
And in the gate at Ancona, between the foregate
And the main-gates
Sigismundo, ally, come through an enemy force,
To patch up some sort of treaty, passes one gate
And they shut it before they open the next gate, and he says:
" Now you have me,
             Caught like a hen in a coop."
And the captain of the watch says: " Yes Messire Sigismundo,
But we want this town for ourselves."

With the church against him,
With the Medici bank for itself,
With wattle Sforza against him
Sforza Francesco, wattle-nose,
Who married him (Sigismundo) his (Francesco's)
Daughter in September,
Who stole Pèsaro in October (as Broglio says "*bestialmente*"),
Who stood with the Venetians in November,
With the Milanese in December,
Sold Milan in November, stole Milan in December
Or something of that sort,
Commanded the Milanese in the spring,
the Venetians at midsummer,
The Milanese in the autumn,
And was Naples' ally in October,
      He, Sigismundo, *templum ædificavit*
In Romagna, teeming with cattle thieves,
      with the game lost in mid-channel,
And never quite lost till' 50,
      and never quite lost till the end, in Romagna,
So that Galeaz sold Pèsaro " to get pay for his cattle."

And Poictiers, you know, Guillaume Poictiers,
      had brought the song up out of Spain
With the singers and viels. But here they wanted a setting,
By Marecchia, where the water comes down over the cobbles
And Mastin had come to Verucchio,
      and the sword, Paolo il Bello's,
      caught in the arras
And, in Este's house, Parisina
Paid
For this tribe paid always, and the house
Called also Atreides',
And the wind is still for a little

And the dusk rolled
            to one side a little
And he was twelve at the time, Sigismundo,
And no dues had been paid for three years,
And his elder brother gone pious;
And that year they fought in the streets,
And that year he got out to Cesena
            And brought back the levies,
And that year he crossed by night over Foglia, and...

IX

ONE year floods rose,
   One year they fought in the snows,
   One year hail fell, breaking the trees and walls.
   Down here in the marsh they trapped him
   in one year,
And he stood in the water up to his neck
   to keep the hounds off him,
And he floundered about in the marsh
   and came in after three days,
That was Astorre Manfredi of Faenza
   who worked the ambush
   and set the dogs off to find him,
In the marsh, down here under Mantua,
And he fought in Fano, in a street fight,
   and that was nearly the end of him;
And the Emperor came down and knighted us,
And they had a wooden castle set up for fiesta,
And one year Basinio went out into the courtyard
   Where the lists were, and the palisades
   had been set for the tourneys,
And he talked down the anti-Hellene,
   And there was an heir male to the seignor,
   And Madame Genevra died.
And he, Sigismundo, was Capitan for the Venetians.
And he had sold off small castles
   and built the great Rocca to his plan,
And he fought like ten devils at Monteluro
   and got nothing but the victory
And old Sforza bitched us at Pèsaro;
   (sic) March the 16th:
" that Messire Alessandro Sforza
   is become lord of Pesaro

34

through the wangle of the Illus. Sgr. Mr. Fedricho d'Orbino
Who worked the wangle with Galeaz
        through the wiggling of Messer Francesco,
Who waggled it so that Galeaz should sell Pesaro
        to Alex and Fossembrone to Feddy;
and he hadn't the right to sell.
And this he did *bestialmente;* that is Sforza did *bestialmente*
as he had promised him, Sigismundo, *per capitoli*
        to see that he, Malatesta, should have Pesaro "
And this cut us off from our south half
        and finished our game, thus, in the beginning,
And he, Sigismundo, spoke his mind to Francesco
        and we drove them out of the Marches.

And the King o' Ragona, Alphonse le roy d'Aragon,
        was the next nail in our coffin,
And all you can say is, anyway,
that he Sigismundo called a town council
And Valturio said " as well for a sheep as a lamb "
        and this change-over (*hæc traditio*)
As old bladder said *" rem eorum saluavit "*
Saved the Florentine state; and that, maybe, was something.
And " Florence our natural ally " as they said in the meeting
        for whatever that was worth afterward.
And he began building the TEMPIO,
        and Polixena, his second wife, died.
And the Venetians sent down an ambassador
And said " speak humanely,
But tell him it's no time for raising his pay."
And the Venetians sent down an ambassador
        with three pages of secret instructions
To the effect: Did he think the campaign was a joy-ride?
And old Wattle-wattle slipped into Milan
But he couldn't stand Sidg being so high with the Venetians
And he talked it over with Feddy; and Feddy said " Pesaro "

And old Foscari wrote " *Caro mio*
" If we split with Francesco you can have it
" And we'll help you in every way possible."
   But Feddy offered it sooner.
And Sigismundo got up a few arches,
And stole that marble in Classe, " stole " that is,
Casus est talis:
   Foscari doge, to the prefect of Ravenna
" Why, what, which, thunder, damnation???? "

Casus est talis:
   Filippo, commendatary of the abbazia
Of Sant Apollinaire, Classe, Cardinal of Bologna
That he did one night (*quadam nocte*) sell to the
Illmo D°, D° Sigismund Malatesta
Lord of Arimnium, marble, porphyry, serpentine,
Whose men, Sigismundo's, came with more than an hundred
two wheeled ox carts and deported, for the beautifying
of the *tempio* where was Santa Maria in Trivio
Where the same are now on the walls. Four hundred
ducats to be paid back to the *abbazia* by the said swindling
Cardinal or his heirs.
   grnnh! rrnnh, pthg.
wheels, plaustra, oxen under night-shield,
And on the 13th of August: Aloysius Purtheo,
The next abbot, to Sigismundo, receipt for 200 ducats
Corn-salve for the damage done in that scurry.

And there was the row about that German-Burgundian female
And it was his messianic year, Poliorcetes,
   but he was being a bit too POLUMETIS
And the Venetians wouldn't give him six months vacation.

And he went down to the old brick heap of Pesaro
   and waited for Feddy

And Feddy finally said " I am coming!...
       ... to help Alessandro."
And he said: " This time Mister Feddy has done it."
He said: " Broglio, I'm the goat.   This time
       Mr. Feddy has done it (*m'l'a calata*)."
And he'd lost his job with the Venetians,
And the stone didn't come in from Istria:
And we sent men to the silk war;
And Wattle never paid up on the naíl
       Though we signed on with Milan and Florence;
And he set up the bombards in muck down by Vada
       where nobody else could have set 'em
       and he took the wood out of the bombs
       and made 'em of two scoops of metal
And the jobs getting smaller and smaller,
       Until he signed on with Siena;
       And that time they grabbed his post-bag.
And what was it, anyhow?
       Pitigliano, a man with a ten acre lot,
Two lumps of tufa,
       and they'd taken his pasture land from him,
And Sidg had got back their horses,
       and he had two big lumps of tufa
       with six hundred pigs in the basements.
And the poor devils were dying of cold.
And this is what they found in the post-bag:
       Ex Arimino die xx Decembris
    " *Magnifice ac potens domine, mi singularissime*
" I advise yr. Lordship how
" I have been with master Alwidge who
" has shown me the design of the nave that goes in the middle,
" of the church and the design for the roof and..."
" JHesus,
" *Magnifico exso*.   Signor Mio
" Sence to-day I am recommended that I have to tel you my

37

" father's opinium that he has shode to Mr. Genare about the
" valts of the cherch... etc ...

" Giovane of Master alwise P. S. I think it advisabl that
" I shud go to rome to talk to mister Albert so as I can no
" what he thinks about it rite.

" Sagramoro..."

" *Illustre signor mio*, Messire Battista..."

" First: Ten slabs best red, seven by 15, by one third,
" Eight ditto, good red, 15 by three by one,
" Six of same, 15 by one by one.
" Eight columns 15 by three and one third
              etc... with carriage, danars 151
" MONSEIGNEUR:
    " Madame Isotta has had me write today about Sr. Galeazzo's
" daughter. The man who said young pullets make thin
" soup, knew what he was talking about. We went to see the
" girl the other day, for all the good that did, and she denied
" the whole matter and kept her end up without losing her
" temper. I think Madame Ixotta very nearly exhausted the
" matter. *Mi pare che avea decto hogni chossia.* All the
" children are well. Where you are everyone is pleased and
" happy because of your taking the chateau here we are the
" reverse as you might say drifting without a rudder. Madame
" Lucrezia has probably, or should have, written to you, I
" suppose you have the letter by now. Everyone wants to be
" remembered to you.   21 Dec. D. de M."

" ... *sagramoro* to put up the derricks. There is a supply of
" beams at..."

" MAGNIFICENT LORD WITH DUE REVERENCE:
    " Messire Malatesta is well and asks for you every day. He
" is so much pleased with his pony, It wd. take me a month
" to write you all the fun he gets out of that pony. I want to
" again remind you to write to Georgio Rambottom or to his

" boss to fix up that wall to the little garden that madame Isotta
" uses, for it is all flat on the ground now as I have already told
" him a lot of times, for all the good that does, so I am writing
" to your lordship in the matter I have done all that I can, for
" all the good that does as noboddy hear can do anything
" without you.
                    " your faithful
                                        LUNARDA DA PALLA.
                                        20 Dec. 1454."

" ... gone over it with all the foremen and engineers. And
" about the silver for the small medal..."

" *Magnifice ac poten...*
            " because the walls of..."

" *Malatesta de Malatestis ad Magnificum Dominum Patremque*
" *suum.*

" Ex^{so} D^{no} et D^{no} sin D^{no} Sigismundum Pandolfi Filium
            " Malatestis Capitan General

" Magnificent and Exalted Lord and Father in especial my
" lord with due recommendation: your letter has been pre-
" sented to me by Gentilino da Gradara and with it the bay
" pony (ronzino baiectino) the which you have sent me, and
" which appears in my eyes a fine caparison'd charger, upon
" which I intend to learn all there is to know about riding, in
" consideration of yr. paternal affection for which I thank
" your excellency thus briefly and pray you continue to hold
" me in this esteem notifying you by the bearer of this that
" we are all in good health, as I hope and desire your Ex^{ct}
" Lordship is also: with continued remembrance I remain
            " Your son and servant
                                MALATESTA DE MALATESTIS.
                    Given in Rimini, this the 22nd day of December
                                anno domini 1454 "
                            (*in the sixth year of his age*)

39

"Illustrious Prince:

  "Unfitting as it is that I should offer counsels to Hannibal..."

  "   *Magnifice ac potens domine, domini mi singularissime,*
"*humili recomendatione permissa* etc. This to advise your
"M^{gt} Ld^{shp} how the second load of Veronese marble has
"finally got here, after being held up at Ferrara with no end
"of fuss and botheration, the whole of it having been there
"unloaded.

  "I learned how it happened, and it has cost a few florins to
"get back the said load which had been seized for the skipper's
"debt and defalcation; he having fled when the lighter was
"seized. But that Y^r M^{gt} Ld^{shp} may not lose the moneys
"paid out on his account I have had the lighter brought here
"and am holding it, against his arrival. If not we still have
"the lighter.

  "As soon as the Xmas fêtes are over I will have the stone
"floor laid in the sacresty, for which the stone is already cut.
"The wall of the building is finished and I shall now get the
"roof on.

  "We have not begun putting new stone into the martyr
"chapel; first because the heavy frosts wd. certainly spoil
"the job; secondly because the aliofants aren't yet here and
"one can't get the measurements for the cornice to the columns
"that are to rest on the aliofants.

  "They are doing the stairs to your room in the castle... I
"have had Messire Antonio degli Atti's court paved and the
"stone benches put in it.

  "Ottavian is illuminating the bull. I mean the bull for
"the chapel. All the stone-cutters are waiting for spring
"weather to start work again.

  "The tomb is all done except part of the lid, and as soon as
"Messire Agostino gets back from Cesena I will see that he
"finishes it, ever recommending me to y^r M^{gt} Ld^{shp}

                              "believe me y^r faithful
                              Petrus Genariis."

That's what they found in the post-bag
And some more of it to the effect that
        he " lived and ruled "

" *et amava perdutamente Ixotta degli Atti* "
e " *ne fu degna* "
            " *constans in proposito*
" *Placuit oculis principis*
" *pulchra aspectu* "
" *populo grata (Italiaeque decus)*
" and built a temple so full of pagan works "
        i. e. Sigismund
and in the style " Past ruin'd Latium "
The filagree hiding the gothic,
        with a touch of rhetoric in the whole
And the old sarcophagi,
        such as lie, smothered in grass, by San Vitale.

X

AND the poor devils dying of cold, outside Sorano,
And from the other side, from inside the château,
Orsini, Count Pitigliano, on the 17th of November:
"Siggy, darlint, wd. you not stop making war on
"insensible objects, such as trees and domestic vines, that have
"no means to hit back... but if you will hire yourself out to a
"commune (Siena) which you ought rather to rule than
"serve..."
    which with Trachulo's damn'd epistle...
And what of it *any*how? a man with a ten acre lot,
Pitigliano... a lump of tufa,
        And S. had got back their horses
And the poor devils dying of cold...
(And there was another time, you know,
He signed on with the Fanesi,
        and just couldn't be bothered...)
And there were three men on a one man job
        And Careggi wanting the baton,
And not getting it just then in any case.

And he, Sigismundo, refused an invitation to lunch
        In commemoration of Carmagnola
        (vide Venice, between the two columns
        where Carmagnola was executed.)
        Et
        "*anno messo a saccho el signor Sigismundo*"
As Filippo Strozzi wrote to Zan Lottieri, then in Naples,
        "I think they'll let him through at Campiglia"

        Florence, Archivio Storico, 4th Series t. iii, e
        "*La Guerra dei Senesi col conte di Pitigliano.*"

And he found Carlo Gonzaga sitting like a mud-frog
        in Orbetello

And he said:
> "*Caro mio,* I can not receive you
It really *is* not the moment."
And Broglio says he ought to have tipped Gorro Lolli.
But he got back home here somehow,
And Piccinino was out of a job,
And the old row with Naples continued.
And what he said was all right in Mantua;
And Borso had the pair of them up to Bel Fiore,
The pair of them, Sigismundo and Federico Urbino,
Or perhaps in the palace, Ferrara, Sigismund upstairs
And Urbino's gang in the basement,
And a regiment of guards in, to keep order,
> For all the good that did:
"*Te cavero la budella del corpo!*"
El conte levatosi:
> "*Io te cavero la corata a te!*"
And that day Cosimo smiled,
That is, the day they said:
> "Drusiana is to marry Count Giacomo..."
(Piccinino) *un sorriso malizioso.*
Drusiana, another of Franco Sforza's;
It would at least keep the row out of Tuscany.
And he fell out of a window, Count Giacomo,
Three days after his death, that was years later in Naples,
For trusting Ferdinando of Naples,
And old Wattle could do nothing about it.

Et:

. . . .
INTEREA PRO GRADIBUS BASILICAE S. PIETRI EX ARIDA MATERIA
INGENS PYRA EXTRUITUR IN CUJUS SUMMITATE IMAGO SIGIS-
MUNDI COLLOCATUR HOMINIS LINEAMENTA, ET VESTIMENTI
MODUM ADEO PROPRIE REDDENS, UT VERA MAGIS PERSONA,
QUAM IMAGO VIDERETUR; NE QUEM TAMEN IMAGO FALLERET,

43

ET SCRIPTURA EX ORE PRODIIT, QUAE DICERET:
    SIGISMUNDUS HIC EGO SUM
MALATESTA, FILIUS PANDULPHI, REX PRODITORUM,
DEO ATQUE HOMINIBUS INFESTUS, SACRI CENSURA SENATUS
IGNI DAMNATUS;

                                    SCRIPTURUM.
MULTI LEGERUNT. DEINDE ASTANTE POPULO, IGNI IMMISSO,
ET PYRA SIMULACRUM REPENTE FLAGRAVIT.

                        Com. Pio II, Liv. VII, p. 85.
                        Yriarte, p. 288.

. . . .

So that in the end that pot-scraping little runt Andreas
        Benzi, da Siena
Got up to spout out the bunkum
That that monstrous swollen, swelling s. o. b.
        Papa Pio Secundo
        Æneas Silvius Piccolomini
        da Siena
Had told him to spout, in their best bear's-greased latinity;

Stupro, cæde, adulter,
homocidia, parricidia ac periurus,
presbitericidia, audax, libidinosus,
wives, jew-girls, nuns, necrophiliast, *fornicarium ac sicarium,*
proditor, raptor, incestuosus, incendiarius, ac
concubinarius,
and that he rejected the whole symbol of the apostles,
and that he said the monks ought not to own property
and that he disbelieved in the temporal power,
neither christian, jew, gentile,
        nor any sect pagan, *nisi forsitan epicureæ.*

And that he did among other things
Empty the fonts of the chiexa of holy water
And fill up the same full with ink

That he might in God's dishonour
Stand before the doors of the said chiexa
Making mock of the inky faithful, they
Issuing thence by the doors in the pale light of the sunrise
Which might be considered youthful levity
        but was really a profound indication;

" Whence that his, Sigismundo's, fœtor filled the earth
And stank up through the air and stars to heaven
Where — save they were immune from sufferings —
It had made the emparadisèd spirits pewk "
        from their jeweled terrace.

" *Lussurioso incestuoso, perfide, sozzure ac crapulone,*
assassino, ingordo, avaro, superbo, infidele
fattore di monete false, sodomitico, uxoricido "

and the whole lump lot
given over to...

I mean after Pio had said, or at least Pio says that he
Said that this was elegant oratory " *Orationem*
Elegantissimam et ornatissimam
Audivimus venerabilis in Xti fratres ac dilectissimi
filii... (stone in his bladder
        testibus idoneis)
The lump lot given over
To that kid-slapping fanatic il cardinale di San Pietro in Vincoli
        To find him guilty, of the lump lot
As he duly did, calling rumour, and Messire Federico d'Urbino
And other equally unimpeachable witnesses.

So they burnt our brother in effigy
A rare magnificent effigy costing 8 florins 48 bol
(i.e. for the pair, as the first one wasn't a good enough likeness)
And Borso said the time was ill-suited
        to *tanta novità,* such doings or innovations,

45

God's enemy and man's enemy, *stuprum, raptum*
	I. N. R. I. Sigismund Imperator, Rex Proditorum.

And old Pills who tried to get him into a front rank action
In order to drive the rear guard at his buttocks,
Old Pills listed among the murdered, although he
Came out of jail living later.

Et les angloys ne povans desraciner... venin de hayne
Had got back Gisors from the Angevins,

And the Angevins were gunning after Naples
And we dragged in the Angevins,
And we dragged in Louis Eleventh,
And the *tiers Calixte* was dead, and Alfonso;
And against us we had " this Æneas " and young Ferdinando
That we had smashed at Piombino and driven out of the
Terrene of the Florentines;
And Piccinino, out of a job;
And he, Sidg, had had three chances of
Making it up with Alfonso, and an offer of
Marriage alliance;

And what he said was all right there in Mantua;
But Pio, sometime or other, Pio lost his pustulous temper.
And they struck alum at Tolfa, in the pope's land,
	To pay for their devilment.
And Francesco said:
	I also have suffered.
When you take it, give me a slice.
	And they nearly jailed a chap for saying
The job was *mal hecho;* and they caught poor old Pasti
In Venice, and were like to pull all his teeth out;
And they had a bow-shot at Borso
As he was going down the Grand Canal in his gondola
	(the nice kind with 26 barbs on it)

46

And they said: Novvy'll sell any man
        for the sake of Count Giacomo.
(Piccinino, the one that fell out of the window).

And they came at us with their ecclesiastical legates
Until the eagle lit on his tent pole.
And he said: The Romans would have called that an augury
E gradment li antichi cavaler romanj
        davano fed a quisti annutii,
All I want you to do is to follow the orders,
They've got a bigger army,
        but there are more men in this camp.

XI

EGRADMENT *li antichi cavaler romanj*
                davano fed a quisti annutii
        And he put us under the chiefs,
                and the chiefs went back to their squadrons:
Bernardo Reggio, Nic Benzo, Giovan Nestorno,
Paulo Viterbo, Buardino of Brescia,
                Cetho Brandolino,
And Simone Malespina, Petracco Saint Archangelo,
Rioberto da Canossa,
And for the tenth Agniolo da Roma
                And that gay bird Piero della Bella,
And to the eleventh Roberto,
And the papishes were three thousand on horses,
dilly cavalli tre milia,
And a thousand on foot,
And the Lord Sigismundo had but mille tre cento cavalli
And hardly 500 fanti (and one spingard),
And we beat the papishes and fought
them back through the tents
And he came up to the dyke again
And fought through the dyke-gate
And it went on from dawn to sunset
And we broke them and took their baggage
                and mille cinquecento cavalli
E li homini di Messire Sigismundo
non furono che mille trecento

And the Venetians sent in their compliments
And various and sundry sent in their compliments;
But we got it next August;
And Roberto got beaten at Fano,
And he went by ship to Tarentum,

48

I mean Sidg went to Tarentum
And he found 'em, the anti-Aragons,
              busted and weeping into their beards.
And they, the papishes, came up to the walls,
And that nick-nosed s.o.b. Feddy Urbino
Said: " *Par che e fuor di questo . . . Sigis . . . mundo.* "
" They say he dodders about the streets
" And can put his hand to neither one thing nor the other,"
And he was in the sick wards, and on the high tower
And everywhere, keeping us at it.
And, thank God, they got the sickness outside
As we had the sickness inside,
And they had neither town nor castello
But dey got de mos' bloody rottenes' peace on us —
Quali lochi sono questi:
              Sogliano,
Torrano and La Serra, Sbrigara, San Martino,
Ciola, Pondo, Spinello, Cigna and Buchio,
Prataline, Monte Cogruzzo,
              and the villa at Rufiano
Right up to the door-yard
And anything else the Rev^{mo} Monsignore could remember.
And the water-rights on the Savio.
(And the salt heaps with the reed mats on them
              Gone long ago to the Venetians)
And when lame Novvy died, they got even Cesena.

And he wrote to young Piero:
              Send me a couple of huntin' dogs,
They may take my mind off it.
And one day he was sitting in the chiexa,
On a bit of cornice, a bit of stone grooved for a cornice,
Too narrow to fit his big beam,
              hunched up and noting what was done wrong,

And an old woman came in and giggled to see him
                    sitting there in the dark
She nearly fell over him,
                    And he thought:
Old Zuliano is finished,
If he's left anything we must see the kids get it,
Write that to Robert.
And Vanni must give that peasant a decent price for his horses,
Say that I will refund.

And the writs run in Fano,
For the long room over the arches
Sub annulo piscatoris, palatium seu curiam OLIM *de Malatestis.*
Gone, and Cesena, Zezena *d'"e b'"e colonne,*
And the big diamond pawned in Venice,
And he gone out into Morea,
Where they sent him to do in the Mo'ammeds,
With 5,000 against 25,000,
                    and he nearly died out in Sparta,
Morea, Lakedæmon,
                    and came back with no pep in him
And we sit here.   I have sat here
                    For forty four thousand years,
And they trapped him down here in the marsh land,
                    in '46 that was;
And the poor devils dying of cold, that was Rocca Sorano;
And he said in his young youth:
                    Vogliamo,
che le donne, we will that they, *le donne,* go ornate,
As be their pleasure, for the city's glory thereby.

And Platina said afterward,
                    when they jailed him
And the Accademia Romana,
For singing to Zeus in the catacombs,

Yes, I saw him when he was down here
Ready to murder fatty Barbo, "Formosus,"
And they want to know what we talked about?
　　　　" *de litteris et de armis, praestantibusque ingeniis,*
Both of ancient times and our own; books, arms,
And of men of unusual genius,
Both of ancient times and our own, in short the usual subjects
Of conversation between intelligent men."

And he with his luck gone out of him
64 lances in his company, and his pay 8,000 a *year,*
64 and no more, and he not to try to get any more
And all of it down on paper
sexaginta quatuor nec tentatur habere plures
But leave to keep 'em in Rimini
　　　　i.e. to watch the Venetians.

Damn pity he didn't
　　　　(i.e. get the knife into him)
Little fat squab " Formosus "
Barbo said " Call me Formosus "
But the conclave wouldn't have it
　　　　and they called him Paolo Secondo.

And he left three horses at one gate
　　　　And three horses at the other,
And Fatty received him
　　　　with a guard of seven cardinals " whom he could trust."
And the castelan of Montefiore wrote down,
" You'd better keep him out of the district.
" When he got back here from Sparta, the people
" Lit fires, and turned out yelling: ' PANDOLFO '! "

In the gloom, the gold gathers the light against it.

And one day he said: Henry, you can have it,
On condition, you can have it: for four months
You'll stand any reasonable joke that I play on you,
And you can joke back
              provided you don't get too ornry.
And they put it all down in writing:
For a green cloak with silver brocade
Actum in Castro Sigismundo, presente Roberto de Valturibus
.. sponte et ex certa scienta... to Enricho de Aquabello.

XII

AND we sit here
                under the wall,
        Arena romana, Diocletian's, les gradins
                quarante-trois rangées en calcaire.
Baldy Bacon
        bought all the little copper pennies in Cuba:
Un centavo, dos centavos,
        told his peons to " bring 'em in."
" Bring 'em to the main shack," said Baldy,
And the peons brought 'em;
" to the main shack brought 'em,"
As Henry would have said.
        Nicholas Castano in Habana,
He also had a few centavos, but the others
Had to pay a percentage.
        Percentage when they wanted centavos,
Public centavos.
        Baldy's interest
Was in money business.
        " No interest in any other kind uv bisnis,"
Said Baldy.
        Sleeping with two buck niggers chained to him,
Guardia regia, chained to his waist
To keep 'em from slipping off in the night;
Being by now unpopular with the Cubans;
        By fever reduced to lbs. 108.
Returned to Manhattan, ultimately to Manhattan.
24 E. 47th, when I met him,
Doing job printing, i.e., agent,
        going to his old acquaintances,
His office in Nassau St., distributing jobs to the printers,

Commercial stationery,
        and later, insurance,
Employers' liability,
        odd sorts of insurance,
Fire on brothels, etc., commission,
Rising from 15 dollars a week,
        Pollon d'anthropon iden,
Knew which shipping companies were most careless;
        where a man was most likely
To lose a leg in bad hoisting machinery;
Also fire, as when passing a whore-house,
Arrived, miraculous Hermes, by accident,
Two minutes after the proprietor's *angelos*
Had been sent for him.
Saved his people 11,000 in four months
        on that Cuba job,
But they busted,
Also ran up to 40,000 bones on his own,
   Once, but wanted to " eat up the whole'r Wall St."
And dropped it all three weeks later.
Habitat cum Quade, damn good fellow,
Mons Quade who wore a monocle on a wide sable ribbon.
        (Elsewhere recorded).
Dos Santos, José Maria dos Santos,
Hearing that a grain ship
Was wrecked in the estuary of the Tagus,
Bought it at auction, nemo obstabat,
No one else bidding. " Damn fool! " " Maize
Spoiled with salt water,
No use, can't do anything with it." Dos Santos.
All the stuff rotted with sea water.
Dos Santos Portuguese lunatic bought it,
Mortgaged then all his patrimony,
        e tot lo sieu aver,
And bought sucking pigs, pigs, small pigs,

Porkers, throughout all Portugal,
        fed on the cargo,
First lot mortgaged to buy the second lot, undsoweiter,
Porkers of Portugal,
        fattening with the fulness of time,
And Dos Santos fattened, a great landlord of Portugal
Now gathered to his fathers.
        Did it on water-soaked corn.
(Water probably fresh in that estuary)
Go to hell Apovitch, Chicago aint the whole punkin.
    Jim X...
        in a bankers' meeting,
        bored with their hard luck stories,
Bored with their bloomin' primness
        and the little white rims
They wore around inside the edge of their vests
To make 'em look as if they had on two waistcoats,
Told 'em the Tale of the Honest Sailor.
Bored with their proprieties,
        as they sat, the ranked presbyterians,
Directors, dealers through holding companies,
Deacons in churches, owning slum properties,
Alias usurers in excelsis,
        the quintessential essence of usurers,
The purveyors of employment, whining over their 20 p. c.
        and the hard times,
And the bust-up of Brazilian securities
        (S. A. securities),
And the general uncertainty of all investment
Save investment in new bank buildings,
        productive of bank buildings,
And not likely to ease distribution,
Bored with the way their mouths twitched
        over their cigar-ends,

Said Jim X... :

There once was a pore honest sailor, a heavy drinker,
A hell of a cuss, a rowster, a boozer, and
The drink finally sent him to hospital,
And they operated, and there was a poor whore in
The woman's ward had a kid, while
They were fixing the sailor, and they brought him the kid
When he came to, and said:
        " Here! this is what we took out of you."

An' he looked at it, an' he got better,
And when he left the hospital, quit the drink,
And when he was well enough
                signed on with another ship
And saved up his pay money,
                and kept on savin' his pay money,
And bought a share in the ship,
                and finally had half shares,
Then a ship
                and in time a whole line of steamers;
And educated the kid,
                and when the kid was in college,
The ole sailor was again taken bad
                and the doctors said he was dying,
And the boy came to the bedside,
                and the old sailor said:
" Boy, I'm sorry I can't hang on a bit longer,
" You're young yet.
                I leave you re-sponsa-bilities.
" Wish I could ha' waited till you were older,
" More fit to take over the bisness..."
                " But, father,
" Don't, don't talk about me, I'm all right,
" It's you, father."
                " That's it, boy, you said it.

" You called me your father, and I ain't.
" I ain't your dad, no,
" I am not your fader but your moder," quod he,
" Your fader was a rich merchant in Stambouli."

XIII

Kung walked
    by the dynastic temple
    and into the cedar grove,
        and then out by the lower river,
And with him Khieu Tchi
        and Tian the low speaking
And " we are unknown," said Kung,
" You will take up charioteering?
        Then you will become known,
" Or perhaps I should take up charioteering, or archery?
" Or the practice of public speaking? "
And Tseu-lou said, " I would put the defences in order,"
And Khieu said, " If I were lord of a province
I would put it in better order than this is."
And Tchi said, " I would prefer a small mountain temple,
" With order in the observances,
        with a suitable performance of the ritual,"
And Tian said, with his hand on the strings of his lute
The low sounds continuing·
        after his hand left the strings,
And the sound went up like smoke, under the leaves,
And he looked after the sound:
        " The old swimming hole,
" And the boys flopping off the planks,
" Or sitting in the underbrush playing mandolins."
        And Kung smiled upon all of them equally.
And Thseng-sie desired to know:
        " Which had answered correctly? "
And Kung said, " They have all answered correctly,
" That is to say, each in his nature."
And Kung raised his cane against Yuan Jang,
        Yuan Jang being his elder,.

For Yuan Jang sat by the roadside pretending to
        be receiving wisdom.
And Kung said
        " You old fool, come out of it,
Get up and do something useful."
        And Kung said
" Respect a child's faculties
" From the moment it inhales the clear air,
" But a man of fifty who knows nothing
        Is worthy of no respect."
And " When the prince has gathered about him
" All the savants and artists, his riches will be fully employed."
And Kung said, and wrote on the bo leaves:
        If a man have not order within him
He can not spread order about him;
And if a man have not order within him
His family will not act with due order;
        And if the prince have not order within him
He can not put order in his dominions.
And Kung gave the words " order "
and " brotherly deference "
And said nothing of the " life after death."
And he said
        " Anyone can run to excesses,
It is easy to shoot past the mark,
It is hard to stand firm in the middle."

And they said: If a man commit murder
        Should his father protect him, and hide him?
And Kung said:
        He should hide him.

And Kung gave his daughter to Kong-Tch'ang
        Although Kong-Tch'ang was in prison.
And he gave his niece to Nan-Young
        although Nan-Young was out of office.

And Kung said " Wang ruled with moderation,
       In his day the State was well kept,
And even I can remember
A day when the historians left blanks in their writings,
I mean for things they didn't know,
But that time seems to be passing."
And Kung said, " Without character you will
       be unable to play on that instrument
Or to execute the music fit for the Odes.
The blossoms of the apricot
       blow from the east to the west,
And I have tried to keep them from falling. "

XIV

Io venni in luogo d'ogni luce muto;
    The stench of wet coal, politicians
    . . . . e and . . . . . n, their wrists bound to
       their ankles,
Standing bare bum,
Faces smeared on their rumps,
        wide eye on flat buttock,
Bush hanging for beard,
    Addressing crowds through their arse-holes,
Addressing the multitudes in the ooze,
       newts, water-slugs, water-maggots,
And with them. . . . . . r,
      a scrupulously clean table-napkin
Tucked under his penis,
      and . . . . m
Who disliked colloquial language,
Stiff-starched, but soiled, collars
      circumscribing his legs,
The pimply and hairy skin
      pushing over the collar's edge,
Profiteers drinking blood sweetened with sh-t,
And behind them . . . . . f and the financiers
    lashing them with steel wires.

And the betrayers of language
      . . . . . . n and the press gang
And those who had lied for hire;
the perverts, the perverters of language,
      the perverts, who have set money-lust
Before the pleasures of the senses;

howling, as of a hen-yard in a printing-house,
    the clatter of presses,

the blowing of dry dust and stray paper,
fœtor, sweat, the stench of stale oranges,
dung, last cess-pool of the universe,
mysterium, acid of sulphur,
the pusillanimous, raging;
plunging jewels in mud,
       and howling to find them unstained;
sadic mothers driving their daughters to bed with decrepitude,
sows eating their litters,
and here the placard ΕΙΚΩΝ ΓΗΣ,
      and here: THE PERSONNEL CHANGES,

melting like dirty wax,
      decayed candles, the bums sinking lower,
faces submerged under hams,
And in the ooze under them,
reversed, foot-palm to foot-palm,
      hand-palm to hand-palm, the agents provocateurs
The murderers of Pearse and MacDonagh,
      Captain H. the chief torturer;
The petrified turd that was Verres,
      bigots, Calvin and St. Clement of Alexandria!
black-beetles, burrowing into the sh-t,
The soil a decrepitude, the ooze full of morsels,
lost contours, erosions.

      Above the hell-rot
the great arse-hole,
      broken with piles,
hanging stalactites,
      greasy as sky over Westminster,
the invisible, many English,
      the place lacking in interest,
last squalor, utter decrepitude,

the vice-crusaders, fahrting through silk,
        waving the Christian symbols,
. . . . frigging a tin penny whistle,
Flies carrying news, harpies dripping sh-t through the air,

The slough of unamiable liars,
        bog of stupidities,
malevolent stupidities, and stupidities,
the soil living pus, full of vermin,
dead maggots begetting live maggots,
        slum owners,
usurers squeezing crab-lice, pandars to authority,
pets-de-loup, sitting on piles of stone books,
obscuring the texts with philology,
        hiding them under their persons,
the air without refuge of silence,
        the drift of lice, teething,
and above it the mouthing of orators,
        the arse-belching of preachers.
        And Invidia,
the corruptio, fœtor, fungus,
liquid animals, melted ossifications,
slow rot, fœtid combustion,
    chewed cigar-butts, without dignity, without tragedy,
. . . . .m Episcopus, waving a condom full of black-beetles,
monopolists, obstructors of knowledge.
        obstructors of distribution.

XV

THE saccharescent, lying in glucose,
 the pompous in cotton wool
   with a stench like the fats at Grasse,
 the great scabrous arse-hole, sh-tting flies,
  rumbling with imperialism,
ultimate urinal, middan, pisswallow without a cloaca,
. . . . . . r less rowdy, ... Episcopus
   . . . . sis,
  head down, screwed into the swill,
his legs waving and pustular,
   a clerical jock strap hanging back over the navel
his condom full of black beetles,
  tattoo marks round the anus,
and a circle of lady golfers about him.·

the courageous violent
  slashing themselves with knives,
the cowardly inciters to violence
. . . . . n and. . . . . . . .h eaten by weevils,
. . . . ll like a swollen fœtus,
  the beast with a hundred legs, USURIA
and the swill full of respecters,
  bowing to the lords of the place,
explaining its advantages,
  and the laudatores temporis acti
claiming that the sh-t used to be blacker and richer
and the fabians crying for the petrification of putrefaction,
for a new dung-flow cut in lozenges,
the conservatives chatting,
  distinguished by gaiters of slum-flesh,
and the back-scratchers in a great circle,
  complaining of insufficient attention,

the search without end, counterclaim for the missing scratch
the litigious,
a green bile-sweat, the news owners, ... s
            the anonymous
    . . . . ffe, broken
            his head shot like a cannon-ball toward the glass gate,
peering through it an instant,
            falling back to the trunk, epileptic,
et nulla fidentia inter eos,
            all with their twitching backs,
with daggers, and bottle ends, waiting an
            unguarded moment;

a stench, stuck in the nostrils;
beneath one
            nothing that might not move,
mobile earth, a dung hatching obscenities,
            inchoate error,
boredom born out of boredom,
british weeklies, copies of the . . . . c,
a multiple . . . . . . nn,
and I said, " How is it done? "
            and my guide:
This sort breeds by scission,
This is the fourmillionth tumour.
In this *bolge* bores are gathered,
Infinite pus flakes, scabs of a lasting pox.

skin-flakes, repetitions, erosions,
endless rain from the arse-hairs,
as the earth moves, the centre
        passes over all parts in succession,
a continual bum-belch
            distributing its productions.

Andiamo!
      One's feet sunk,
the welsh of mud gripped one, no hand-rail,
the bog-suck like a whirl-pool,
and he said:
      Close the pores of your feet!
And my eyes clung to the horizon,
      oil mixing with soot;
and again Plotinus:
      To the door,
Keep your eyes on the mirror.
Prayed we to the Medusa,
      petrifying the soil by the shield,
Holding it downward
      he hardened the track
Inch before us, by inch,
      the matter resisting,
The heads rose from the shield,
      hissing, held downwards.
Devouring maggots,
      the face only half potent,
The serpents' tongues
      grazing the swill top,
Hammering the souse into hardness,
      the narrow rast,
Half the width of a sword's edge.
      By this through the dern evil,
now sinking, now clinging,
      Holding the unsinkable shield.
Oblivion,
      forget how long,
sleep, fainting nausea.
      " Whether in Naishapur or Babylon "
I heard in the dream.
      Plotinus gone,

And the shield tied under me, woke;
The gate swung on its hinges;
Panting like a sick dog, staggered,
Bathed in alkali, and in acid.
'Ηέλιον τ' 'Ηέλιον
      blind with the sunlight,
Swollen-eyed, rested,
      lids sinking, darkness unconscious.

XVI

AND before hell mouth; dry plain
             and two mountains;
          On the one mountain, a running form,
             and another
In the turn of the hill; in hard steel
The road like a slow screw's thread,
The angle almost imperceptible,
             so that the circuit seemed hardly to rise;
And the running form, naked, Blake,
Shouting, whirling his arms, the swift limbs,
Howling against the evil,
             his eyes rolling,
Whirling like flaming cart-wheels,
             and his head held backward to gaze on the evil
As he ran from it,
             to be hid by the steel mountain,
And when he showed again from the north side;
             his eyes blazing toward hell mouth,
His neck forward,
             and like him Peire Cardinal.
And in the west mountain, Il Fiorentino,
Seeing hell in his mirror,
             and lo Sordels
Looking on it in his shield;
And Augustine, gazing toward the invisible.

And past them, the criminal
             lying in blue lakes of acid,
The road between the two hills, upward
             slowly,
The flames patterned in lacquer, crimen est actio,
The limbo of chopped ice and saw-dust,

And I bathed myself with the acid to free myself
             of the hell ticks,
Scales, fallen louse eggs.
             Palux Laerna,
the lake of bodies, aqua morta,
of limbs fluid, and mingled, like fish heaped in a bin,
and here an arm upward, clutching a fragment of marble,
And the embryos, in flux,
             new inflow, submerging,
Here an arm upward, trout, submerged by the eels;
             and from the bank, the stiff herbage
the dry nobbled path, saw many known, and unknown,
for an instant;
             submerging,
The face gone, generation.

             Then light air, under saplings,
the blue banded lake under æther,
             an oasis, the stones, the calm field,
the grass quiet,
             and passing the tree of the bough
The grey stone posts,
             and the stair of gray stone,
the passage clean-squared in granite:
             descending,
and I through this, and into the earth,
             patet terra,
entered the quiet air
             the new sky,
the light as after a sun-set,
             and by their fountains, the heroes,
Sigismundo, and Malatesta Novello,
             and founders, gazing at the mounts of their cities.

The plain, distance, and in fount-pools
             the nymphs of that water

rising, spreading their garlands,
          weaving their water reeds with the boughs,
In the quiet,
          and now one man rose from his fountain
and went off into the plain.

Prone in that grass, in sleep;
          et j'entendis des voix:...
                                        wall . . . Strasbourg
Gallifet led that triple charge . . . Prussians
and he said   [*Pharr's narration*]
          it was for the honour of the army.
And they called him a swashbuckler.
          I didn't know what it was
But I thought: This is pretty bloody damn fine.
And my old nurse, he was a man nurse, and
He killed a Prussian and he lay in the street
there in front of our house for three days
And he stank. . . . . . .
          Brother Percy,
And our Brother Percy...
          old Admiral
He was a middy in those days,
And they came into Ragusa
. . . . . place those men went for the Silk War. . . . .
And they saw a procession coming down through
A cut in the hills, carrying something
The six chaps in front carrying a long thing
          on their shoulders,
And they thought it was a funeral,
          but the thing was wrapped up in scarlet,
And he put off in the cutter,
          he was a middy in those days,
To see what the natives were doing,
And they got up to the six fellows in livery,

And they looked at it, and I can still hear the old admiral,
" Was it? it was
       Lord Byron
Dead drunk, with the face of an A y n. . . . .
He pulled it out long, like that:
       the face of an a y n . . . . gel."

And because that son of a bitch,
       Franz Josef of Austria. . . . . .
And because that son of a bitch Napoléon Barbiche...
They put Aldington on Hill 70, in a trench
       dug through corpses
With a lot of kids of sixteen,
Howling and crying for their mamas,
And he sent a chit back to his major:
       I can hold out for ten minutes
With my sergeant and a machine-gun.
       And they rebuked him for levity.
And Henri Gaudier went to it,
       and they killed him,
And killed a good deal of sculpture,
And ole T.E.H. he went to it,
With a lot of books from the library,
London Library, and a shell buried 'em in a dug-out,
And the Library expressed its annoyance.
       And a bullet hit him on the elbow
...gone through the fellow in front of him,
And he read Kant in the Hospital, in Wimbledon,
in the original,
And the hospital staff didn't like it.

And Wyndham Lewis went to it,
With a heavy bit of artillery,
       and the airmen came by with a mitrailleuse,
And cleaned out most of his company,
       and a shell lit on his tin hut,

While he was out in the privvy,
    and he was all there was left of'that outfit.

Windeler went to it,
    and he was out in the Ægæan,
And down in the hold of his ship
    pumping gas into a sausage,
And the boatswain looked over the rail,
    down into amidships, and he said:
    Gees! look a' the Kept'n,
The Kept'n's a-gettin' 'er up.

And Ole Captain Baker went to it,
    with his legs full of rheumatics,
So much so he couldn't run,
    so he was six months in hospital,
Observing the mentality of the patients.

And Fletcher was 19 when he went to it,
And his major went mad in the control pit,
    about midnight, and started throwing the 'phone about
And he had to keep him quiet
    till about six in the morning,
And direct that bunch of artillery.

And Ernie Hemingway went to it,
    too much in a hurry,
And they buried him for four days.

Et ma foi, vous savez,
    tous les nerveux. Non,
Y a une limite; les bêtes, les bêtes ne sont
Pas faites pour ça, c'est peu de chose un cheval.
Les hommes de 34 ans à quatre pattes
    qui criaient " maman." Mais les costauds,
La fin, là à Verdun, n'y avait que ces gros bonshommes
    Et y voyaient extrêmement clair.

Qu'est-ce que ça vaut, les généraux, le lieutenant,
on les pèse à un centigramme,
　　　　　n'y a rien que du bois,
Notr' capitaine, tout, tout ce qu'il y a de plus renfermé
　　　　　de vieux polytechnicien, mais solide,
La tête solide.　Là, vous savez,
Tout, tout fonctionne, et les voleurs, tous les vices,
Mais les rapaces,
　　　　　y avait trois dans notre compagnie, tous tués.
Y sortaient fouiller un cadavre, pour rien,
　　　　　y n'seraient sortis pour rien que ça.
Et les boches, tout ce que vous voulez,
　　　　　militarisme, et cætera, et cætera.
Tout ça, mais, MAIS,
　　　　　l'français, i s'bat quand y a mangé.
Mais ces pauvres types
A la fin y s'attaquaient pour manger,
　　　　　Sans ordres, les bêtes sauvages, on y fait
Prisonniers; ceux qui parlaient français disaient:
　　　　　"Poo quah?　Ma foi on attaquait pour manger."

C'est le corr-ggras, le corps gras,
　　　　　leurs trains marchaient trois kilomètres à l'heure,
Et ça criait, ça grincait, on l'entendait à cinq kilomètres.
(Ça qui finit la guerre.)

　　　　　Liste officielle des morts 5,000,000.

I vous dit, bè, voui, tout sentait le pétrole.
Mais, Non! je l'ai engueulé.
Je lui ai dit:　T'es un con!　T'a raté la guerre.

O voui! tous les hommes de goût, y conviens,
Tout ça en arrière.
　　　　　Mais un mec comme toi!

73

C't homme, un type comme ça!
        Ce qu'il aurait pu encaisser!
Il était dans une fabrique.
What, burying squad, terrassiers, avec leur tête
        en arrière, qui regardaient comme ça,
On risquait la vie pour un coup de pelle,
Faut que ça soit bien carré, exact...

Dey vus a bolcheviki dere, und dey dease him:
Looka vat youah Trotzsk is done, e iss
        madeh deh zhamefull beace!!
"He iss madeh deh zhamefull beace, iss he?
        "He is madeh de zhamevul beace?
"A Brest-Litovsk, yess? Aint yuh herd?
        "He vinneh de vore.
"De droobs iss released vrom de eastern vront, yess?
"Un venn dey getts to deh vestern vront, iss it
        "How many getts dere?
"And dose doat getts dere iss so full off revolutions
"Venn deh vrench is come dhru, yess,
"Dey say, "Vot?" Un de posch say:
        "Aint yeh heard? Say, ve got a rheffolution."

That's the trick with a crowd,
        Get 'em into the street and get 'em moving.
And all the time, there were people going
Down there, over the river.

        There was a man there talking,
To a thousand, just a short speech, and
Then move 'em on. And he said:
Yes, these people, they are all right, they
Can do everything, everything except act;
And go an' hear 'em, but when they are through,
Come to the bolsheviki...

And when it broke, there was the crowd there,
And the cossacks, just as always before,
But one thing, the cossacks said:
        " Pojalouista."
And that got round in the crowd,
And then a lieutenant of infantry
Ordered 'em to fire into the crowd,
        in the square at the end of the Nevsky,
In front of the Moscow station,
And they wouldn't,
And he pulled his sword on a student for laughing,
And killed him,
And a cossack rode out of his squad
On the other side of the square
And cut down the lieutenant of infantry
And that was the revolution...
        as soon as they named it.

And you can't make 'em,
Nobody knew it was coming. They were all ready, the old gang,
Guns on the top of the post-office and the palace,
But none of the leaders knew it was coming.

And there were some killed at the barracks,
But that was between the troops.

So we used to hear it at the opera,
That they wouldn't be under Haig;
        and that the advance was beginning;
That it was going to begin in a week.

XVII

So that the vines burst from my fingers
        And the bees weighted with pollen
        Move heavily in the vine-shoots:
                chirr — chirr — chir-rikk — a purring sound,
And the birds sleepily in the branches.
                ZAGREUS! IO ZAGREUS!
With the first pale-clear of the heaven
And the cities set in their hills,
And the goddess of the fair knees
Moving there, with the oak-woods behind her,
The green slope, with white hounds
                leaping about her;
And thence down to the creek's mouth, until evening,
Flat water before me,
                and the trees growing in water,
Marble trunks out of stillness,
On past the palazzi,
                in the stillness,
The light now, not of the sun.
                Chrysophrase,
And the water green clear, and blue clear;
On, to the great cliffs of amber.
                Between them,
Cave of Nerea,
        she like a great shell curved,
And the boat drawn without sound,
Without odour of ship-work,
Nor bird-cry, nor any noise of wave moving,
Nor splash of porpoise, nor any noise of wave moving,
Within her cave, Nerea,
                she like a great shell curved

In the suavity of the rock,
                    cliff green-gray in the far,
In the near, the gate-cliffs of amber,
And the wave
                    green clear, and blue clear,
And the cave salt-white, and glare-purple,
          cool, porphyry smooth,
          the rock sea-worn.
No gull-cry, no sound of porpoise,
Sand as of malachite, and no cold there,
          the light not of the sun.

Zagreus, feeding his panthers,
          the turf clear as on hills under light.
And under the almond-trees, gods,
          with them, *choros nympharum*. Gods,
Hermes and Athene,
                    As shaft of compass,
Between them, trembled —
To the left is the place of fauns,
                    sylva nympharum;
The low wood, moor-scrub,
          the doe, the young spotted deer,
          leap up through the broom-plants,
                    as dry leaf amid yellow.
And by one cut of the hills,
          the great alley of Memnons.
Beyond, sea, crests seen over dune
Night sea churning shingle,
To the left, the alley of cypress.
                    A boat came,
One man holding her sail,

Guiding her with oar caught over gunwale, saying:
"   There, in the forest of marble,
"   the stone trees — out of water —
"   the arbours of stone —
"   marble leaf, over leaf,
"   silver, steel over steel,
"   silver beaks rising and crossing,
"   prow set against prow,
"   stone, ply over ply,
"   the gilt beams flare of an evening "
Borso, Carmagnola, the men of craft, *i vitrei*,
Thither, at one time, time after time,
And the waters richer than glass,
Bronze gold, the blaze over the silver,
Dye-pots in the torch-light,
The flash of wave under prows,
And the silver beaks rising and crossing.
          Stone trees, white and rose-white in the darkness,
Cypress there by the towers,
          Drift under hulls in the night.

          " In the gloom the gold
Gathers the light about it."...

Now supine in burrow, half over-arched bramble,
One eye for the sea, through that peek-hole,
Gray light, with Athene.
Zothar and her elephants, the gold loin-cloth,
The sistrum, shaken, shaken,
          the cohorts of her dancers.
And Aletha, by bend of the shore,
          with her eyes seaward,
          and in her hands sea-wrack
Salt-bright with the foam.
Koré through the bright meadow,
          with green-gray dust in the grass:

" For this hour, brother of Circe."
Arm laid over my shoulder,
Saw the sun for three days, the sun fulvid,
As a lion lift over sand-plain;
                              and that day,
And for three days, and none after,
Splendour, as the splendour of Hermes,
And shipped thence
                    to the stone place,
Pale white, over water,
                    known water,
And the white forest of marble, bent bough over bough,
The pleached arbour of stone,
Thither Borso, when they shot the barbed arrow at him,
And Carmagnola, between the two columns,
Sigismundo, after that wreck in Dalmatia.
    Sunset like the grasshopper flying.

XVIII

AND of Kublai:
> "I have told you of that emperor's city in detail
> And will tell you of the coining in Cambaluc
> that hyght the secret of alchemy:
They take bast of the mulberry-tree,
That is a skin between the wood and the bark,
And of this they make paper, and mark it
Half a tornesel, a tornesel, or a half-groat of silver,
Or two groats, or five groats, or ten groats,
Or, for a great sheet, a gold bezant, 3 bezants,
> ten bezants;
And they are written on by officials,
And smeared with the great khan's seal in vermilion;
And the forgers are punished with death.
And all this costs the Kahn nothing,
And so he is rich in this world.
And his postmen go sewed up and sealed up,
Their coats buttoned behind and then sealed,
In this way from the voyage's one end to its other.
And the Indian merchants arriving
Must give up their jewels, and take this money
> in paper,
(That trade runs, in bezants, to 400,000 the year.)
And the nobles must buy their pearls "
— thus Messire Polo; prison at Genoa —
" Of the Emperor."
> There was a boy in Constantinople,
And some britisher kicked his arse.
" I hate these french," said Napoleon, aged 12,
To young Bourrienne, " I will do them all the harm
> that I can."
In like manner Zenos Metevsky.

And old Biers was out there, a greenhorn,
To sell cannon, and Metevsky found the back door;
And old Biers sold the munitions,
And Metevsky died and was buried, *i. e.* officially,
And sat in the Yeiner Kafé watching the funeral.
About ten years after this incident,
He owned a fair chunk of Humbers.
                    " Peace! Pieyce!! " said Mr. Giddings,
" Uni-ver-sal? Not while yew got tew billions ov money,"
Said Mr. Giddings, " invested in the man-u-facture
" Of war machinery. Haow I sold it to Russia —
" Well we tuk 'em a new torpedo-boat,
" And it was all electric, run it all from a
" Little bit uv a keyboard, about like the size ov
" A typewriter, and the prince come aboard,
" An' we sez wud yew like to run her?
" And he run damn slam on the breakwater,
" And bust off all her front end,
" And he was my gawd scared out of his panties.
" Who wuz agoin' tew pay fer the damage?
" And it was my first trip out fer the company,
" And I sez, yer highness, it is nothing,
" We will give yew a new one. And, my Christ!
" The company backed me, and did we get a few orders? "
So La Marquesa de las Zojas y Hurbara
Used to drive up to Sir Zenos's place
                    in the Champs Elysées
And preside at his dinners, and at *las once*
She drove away from the front door, with her footmen
And her coachman in livery, and drove four blocks round
To the back door, and her husband was the son of a bitch,
And Metevsky, " the well-known philanthropist,"
Or " the well-known financier, better known,"
As the press said, " as a philanthropist,"
Gave — as the Este to Louis Eleventh, —

81

A fine pair of giraffes to the nation,
And endowed a chair of ballistics,
And was consulted before the offensives.

And Mr. Oige was very choleric in a first-class
From Nice to Paris, he said: " Danger!
" Now a sailor's life is a life of danger,
" But a mine, why every stick of it is numbered,
" And one time we missed one, and there was
" Three hundred men killed in the 'splosion."
He was annoyed with the strikers, having started himself
As engineer and worked up, and losing,
By that coal strike, some months after the paragraph:

: Sir Zenos Metevsky has been elected President
Of the Gethsemane Trebizond Petrol.
And then there came out another: 80 locomotives
On the Manchester Cardiff have been fitted with
New oil-burning apparatus...
Large stocks of the heavier varieties of which (*i. e.* oil)
Are now on hand in the country.

So I said to the old quaker Hamish,
I said: " I am interested." And he went putty colour
And said: " He don't advertise. No, I don't think
You will learn much." That was when I asked
About Metevsky Melchizedek.
He, Hamish, took the tractors up to
King Menelik, 3 rivers and 140 ravines.

" Qu'est-ce qu'on pense...? " I said: " On don't pense.
" They're solid bone. You can amputate from just above
The medulla, and it won't alter the life in that island."
But he continued, " Mais, qu'EST-CE qu'ON pense,
" De la metallurgie, en Angleterre, qu'est-ce qu'on
" Pense de Metevsky? "

And I said: "They ain't heard his name yet.
"Go ask at MacGorvish's bank."

The Jap observers were much amused because
The Turkish freemasons hadn't bothered to
Take the..... regimental badges off their artillery.
And old Hamish: Menelik
Had a hunch that machinery...and so on...
But he never could get it to work,
         never could get any power.
The Germans wd. send him up boilers, but they'd
Have to cut 'em into pieces to load 'em on camels,
And they never got 'em together again.
And so old Hamish went out there,
And looked at the place, 3 rivers
And a hundred and forty ravines,
And he sent out two tractors, one to pull on the other
And Menelik sent down an army, a 5000 black army
With hawsers, and they all sweated and swatted.

And the first thing Dave lit on when they got there
Was a buzz-saw,
And he put it through an ebony log: whhsssh, t ttt,
Two days' work in three minutes.

War, one war after another,
Men start 'em who couldn't put up a good hen-roost.

Also sabotage...

XIX

SABOTAGE? Yes, he took it up to Manhattan,
     To the big company, and they said: Impossible.
     And he said: I gawt ten thousand dollars tew mak 'em,
     And I am a goin' tew mak 'em, and you'll damn well
Have to install 'em, awl over the place.
And they said: Oh, we can't have it.
So he settled for one-half of one million.
And he has a very nice place on the Hudson,
And that invention, patent, is still in their desk.
And the answer to that is: Wa'al he had the ten thousand.
And old Spinder, that put up the 1870 gothick memorial,
He tried to pull me on Marx, and he told me
About the " romance of his business ":
How he came to England with something or other,
                              and sold it.
Only he wanted to talk about Marx, so I sez:
Waal haow is it you're over here, right off the
                              Champz Elyza?
And how can yew be here? Why don't the fellers at home
Take it all off you? How can you leave your big business?
" Oh," he sez, " I ain't had to rent any money...
" It's a long time since I ain't had tew rent any money."
Nawthin' more about Das Kapital,
Or credit, or distribution.
And he " never finished the book,"
That was the other chap, the slender diplomatdentist
Qui se faisait si beau.

So we sat there, with the old kindly professor,
And the stubby little man was up-stairs.
And there was the slick guy in the other

corner reading The Tatler,
Not upside down, but never turning the pages,
And then I went up to the bed-room, and he said,
The stubby fellow: Perfectly true,
" But it's a question of feeling,
" Can't move 'em with a cold thing, like economics."
And so we came down stairs and went out,
And the slick guy looked out of the window,
And in came the street " Lemme-at-'em "
           like a bull-dog in a mackintosh.
           O my Clio!
Then the telephone didn't work for a week.

Ever seen Prishnip, little hunchback,
Couldn't take him for *any* army.
And he said: I haf a messache from dh' professor,
" There's lots of 'em want to go over,
" But when they try to go over,
" Dh' hRussian boys shoot 'em, and they want to know
" How to go over."

Vlettmann?...was out there, and that was,
Say, two months later, and he said:
" Jolly chaps," he said; " they used to go by
" Under my window, at two o'clock in the morning,
" All singing, all singing the *Hé Sloveny!* "

Yes, Vlettmann, and the Russian boys didn't shoot'em.
    Short story, entitled, the Birth of a Nation.
And there was that squirt of an Ausstrrian
        with a rose in his button-hole,
And how the hell he stayed on here,
        right through the whole bhloody business,
Cocky as Khristnoze, and enjoying every Boche victory.
Naphtha, or some damn thing for the submarines,

Like they had, just *had,* to have the hemp
            via Rotterdam.
Das thust du nicht, Albert?
That was in the old days, all sitting around in arm-chairs,
And that's gone, like the cake shops in the Nevsky.
" No use telling 'em anything, revolutionaries,
Till they're at the *end,*
Oh, absolootly, AT the end of their tether.
Governed.   Governed the place from a train,
Or rather from three trains, on a railway,
And he'd keep about three days ahead of the lobby,
I mean he had his government on the trains,
And the lobby had to get there on horseback;
And he said: Bigod it's damn funny,
Own half the oil in the world, and can't get enough
To run a government engine! "
And then they jawed for two hours,
And finally Steff said: Will you fellows show me a map?
And they brought one, and Steff said:
" Waal what are those lines? "   " Yes, those straight lines."
" Those are roads."   And " what are those lines,
" The wiggly ones? "   " Rivers."
And Steff said: " Government property? "

So two hours later an engine went off with the order:
How to dig without confiscation.

And Tommy Baymont said to Steff one day:
" You think we run it, lemme tell you,
" We bought a coalmine, I mean the mortgage fell in,
" And you'd a' thought we could run it.

" Well I had to go down there meself, and the manager
" Said: " Run it, of course we can run it,
" We can't sell the damn coal."

86

So I said to the X. and B. Central,
— you'd say we boss the X. and B. Central? —
I said: You buy your damn coal from our mine.
And a year later they hadn't; so I had up the directors,
And they said:...well anyhow, they couldn't
                              buy the damn coal.
And next week ole Jim came, the big fat one
With the diamonds, and he said: "Mr. Baymont,
You just *must* charge two dollars more
A ton fer that coal.   And the X. and B. will
Take it through us."

" So there was my ole man sitting,
They were in arm-chairs, according to protocol,
And next him his nephew Mr. Wurmsdorf,
And old Ptierstoff, for purely family reasons,
Personal reasons, was held in great esteem
                              by his relatives,
And he had his despatches from St. Petersburg,
And Wurmsdorf had his from Vienna,
And he knew, and they knew, and each knew
That the other knew that the other knew he knew,
And Wurmsdorf was just reaching into his pocket,
That was to start things, and then my ole man
Said it:
              Albert, and the rest of it.
Those days are gone by for ever."

" Ten years gone, ten years of my life,
Never get those ten years back again:
Ten years of my life, ten years in the Indian army;
But anyhow, there was that time in Yash (Jassy):
That was something, 14 girls in a fortnight."
" Healthy but verminous? " " That's it, healthy but verminous.
                              And one time in Kashmir,

In the houseboats, with the turquoise,
A pile three feet high on the boat floor,
And they'd be there all day at a bargain
For ten bobs' worth of turquoise."

XX

Sound slender, quasi tinnula,
    Ligur' aoide: Si no'us vei, Domna don plus mi cal,
    Negus vezer mon bel pensar no val."
    Between the two almond trees flowering,
The viel held close to his side;
And another: s'adora ".
" Possum ego naturae
non meminisse tuae! "   Qui son Properzio ed Ovidio.

The boughs are not more fresh
where the almond shoots
take their March green.
And that year I went up to Freiburg,
And Rennert had said: Nobody, no, nobody
Knows anything about Provençal, or if there is anybody,
It's old Lévy."
And so I went up to Freiburg,
And the vacation was just beginning,
The students getting off for the summer,
Freiburg im Breisgau,
And everything clean, seeming clean, after Italy.

And I went to old Lévy, and it was by then 6.30
in the evening, and he trailed half way across Freiburg
before dinner, to see the two strips of copy,
Arnaut's, settant'uno R. superiore (Ambrosiana)
Not that I could sing him the music.
And he said: Now is there anything I can tell you? "
And I said: I dunno, sir, or
" Yes, Doctor, what do they mean by *noigandres?* "
And he said: Noigandres!   NOIgandres!

"You know for seex mon's of my life
"Effery night when I go to bett, I say to myself:
"Noigandres, eh, *noi*gandres,
"Now what the DEFFIL can that mean!"
Wind over the olive trees, ranunculae ordered,
By the clear edge of the rocks
The water runs, and the wind scented with pine
And with hay-fields under sun-swath.
Agostino, Jacopo and Boccata.
You would be happy for the smell of that place
And never tired of being there, either alone
Or accompanied.
Sound: as of the nightingale too far off to be heard.
Sandro, and Boccata, and Jacopo Sellaio;
The ranunculæ, and almond,
Boughs set in espalier,
Duccio, Agostino; *e l'olors* —
The smell of that place — *d'enoi ganres.*
Air moving under the boughs,
The cedars there in the sun,
Hay new cut on hill slope,
And the water there in the cut
Between the two lower meadows; sound,
The sound, as I have said, a nightingale
Too far off to be heard.
And the light falls, *remir*,
from her breast to thighs.

He was playing there at the palla.
Parisina — two doves for an altar — at the window,
"*E'l Marchese
Stava per divenir pazzo*
after it all." And that was when Troy was down
And they came here and cut holes in rock,
Down Rome way, and put up the timbers;

90

And came here, condit Atesten...
        " Peace! keep the peace, Borso."
And he said: Some bitch has sold us
        (that was Ganelon)
" They wont get another such ivory."
And he lay there on the round hill under the cedar
A little to the left of the cut (Este speaking)
By the side of the summit, and he said:
        "I have broken the horn, bigod, I have
" Broke the best ivory, l'olofans." And he said:
" Tan mare fustes! "
        pulling himself over the gravel,
" Bigod! that buggar is done for,
" They wont get another such ivory."
And they were there before the wall, Toro, las almenas,
(Este, Nic Este speaking)
        Under the battlement
(Epi purgo) peur de la hasle,
And the King said:
        " God what a woman!
My God what a woman " said the King telo rigido.
" Sister! " says Ancures, " 's your sister! "
Alf left that town to Elvira, and Sancho wanted
It from her, Toro and Zamora.
        " Bloody spaniard!
Neestho, le'er go back...
        in the autumn."
" Este, go' damn you." between the walls, arras,
Painted to look like arras.
        Jungle:
Glaze green and red feathers, jungle,
Basis of renewal, renewals;
Rising over the soul, green virid, of the jungle,
Lozenge of the pavement, clear shapes,
Broken, disrupted, body eternal,

Wilderness of renewals, confusion
Basis of renewals, subsistence,
Glazed green of the jungle;
Zoe, Marozia, Zothar,
                    loud over the banners,
Glazed grape, and the crimson,
HO BIOS,
              cosi Elena vedi,
In the sunlight, gate cut by the shadow;
And then the faceted air:
Floating.   Below, sea churning shingle.
Floating, each on invisible raft,
On the high current, invisible fluid,
Borne over the plain, recumbent,
The right arm cast back,
              the right wrist for a pillow,
The left hand like a calyx,
Thumb held against finger, the third,
The first fingers petal'd up, the hand as a lamp,
A calyx.
              From toe to head
The purple, blue-pale smoke, as of incense;
Wrapped each in burnous, smoke as the olibanum's,
Swift, as if joyous.
Wrapped, floating; and the blue-pale smoke of the incense
Swift to rise, then lazily in the wind
              as Aeolus over bean-field,
As hay in the sun, the olibanum, saffron,
As myrrh without styrax;
Each man in his cloth, as on raft, on
              The high invisible current;
On toward the fall of water;
And then over that cataract,
In air, strong, the bright flames, V shaped;
              Nel fuoco

D'amore mi mise, nel fuoco d'amore mi mise...
Yellow, bright saffron, croceo;
And as the olibanum bursts into flame,
The bodies so flamed in the air, took flame,
      "...Mi mise, il mio sposo novello."
Shot from stream into spiral,

Or followed the water. Or looked back to the flowing;
Others approaching that cataract,
As to dawn out of shadow, the swathed cloths
Now purple and orange,
And the blue water dusky beneath them,
      pouring there into the cataract,
With noise of sea over shingle,
        striking with:
          hah hah ahah thmm, thunb, ah
          woh woh araha thumm, bhaaa.
And from the floating bodies, the incense
    blue-pale, purple above them.
Shelf of the lotophagoi,
Aerial, cut in the aether.
            Reclining,
With the silver spilla,
The ball as of melted amber, coiled, caught up, and turned.
Lotophagoi of the suave nails, quiet, scornful,
Voce-profondo:
      "Feared neither death nor pain for this beauty;
If harm, harm to ourselves."
And beneath: the clear bones, far down,
Thousand on thousand.
      "What gain with Odysseus,
" They that died in the whirlpool
" And after many vain labours,
" Living by stolen meat, chained to the rowingbench,
" That he should have a great fame

" And lie by night with the goddess?
" Their names are not written in bronze
        " Nor their rowing sticks set with Elpenor's;
" Nor have they mound by sea-bord.
            " That saw never the olives under Spartha
" With the leaves green and then not green,
        " The click of light in their branches;
" That saw not the bronze hall nor the ingle
" Nor lay there with the queen's waiting maids,
" Nor had they Circe to couch-mate, Circe Titania,
" Nor had they meats of Kalüpso
" Or her silk skirts brushing their thighs.
" Give!   What were they given?
                            Ear-wax.
" Poison and ear-wax,
                and a salt grave by the bull-field,
" *neson amumona*, their heads like sea crows in the foam,
" Black splotches, sea-weed under lightning;
" Canned beef of Apollo, ten cans for a boat load."
Ligur' aoide.

And from the plain whence the water-shoot,
Across, back, to the right, the roads, a way in the grass,
The Khan's hunting leopard, and young Salustio
And Ixotta; the suave turf
Ac ferae familiares, and the cars slowly,
And the panthers, soft-footed.
Plain, as the plain of Somnus,
            the heavy cars, as a triumph,
Gilded, heavy on wheel,
            and the panthers chained to the cars,
Over suave turf, the form wrapped,
Rose, crimson, deep crimson,
And, in the blue dusk, a colour as of rust in the sunlight,
Out of white cloud, moving over the plain,

Head in arm's curve, reclining;
The road, back and away, till cut along the face of the rock,
And the cliff folds in like a curtain,
The road cut in under the rock
Square groove in the cliff's face, as chiostri,
The columns crystal, with peacocks cut in the capitals,
The soft pad of beasts dragging the cars;
Cars, slow, without creak,
And at windows in inner roadside:
        le donne e i cavalieri
         smooth face under hennin,
The sleeves embroidered with flowers,
Great thistle of gold, or an amaranth,
Acorns of gold, or of scarlet,
Cramoisi and diaspre
         slashed white into velvet;
Crystal columns, acanthus, sirens in the pillar heads;
And at last, between gilded barocco,
Two columns coiled and fluted,
Vanoka, leaning half naked,
       waste hall there behind her.
" Peace!
      Borso..., Borso! "

XXI

KEEP the peace, Borso! " Where are we?
    " Keep on with the business,
                That's made me,
    " And the res publica didn't.
" When I was broke, and a poor kid,
" They all knew me, all of these *cittadini,*
" And they all of them cut me dead, della gloria."
Intestate, 1429, leaving 178,221 florins *di sugello,*
As is said in Cosimo's red leather note book.   Di sugello.
And " with his credit emptied Venice of money "—
That was Cosimo —
" And Naples, and made them accept his peace."
And he caught the young boy Ficino
And had him taught the greek language;
" With two ells of red cloth per person
I will make you ", Cosimo speaking, " as many
Honest citizens as you desire."
Col credito suo...
Napoli e Venezia di danari...
Costretti... Napoli e Venezia... a quella pace...
Or another time... oh well, pass it.
And Piero called in the credits,
(Diotisalvi was back of that)
And firms failed as far off as Avignon,
And Piero was like to be murdered,
And young Lauro came down ahead of him, in the road,
And said: Yes, father is coming.

Intestate, '69, in December, leaving me 237,989 florins,
As you will find in my big green account book
In carta di capretto;

And from '34 when I count it, to last year,
We paid out 600,000 and over,
That was for building, taxes and charity.
Nic Uzano saw us coming.   Against it, honest,
And warned 'em.   They'd have murdered him,
And would Cosimo, but he bribed 'em;
And they did in Giuliano.   E difficile,
A Firenze difficile viver ricco
Senza aver lo stato.
" E non avendo stato Piccinino
" Doveva temerlo qualunque era in stato; "
And " that man sweated blood to put through that railway ";
" Could you ", wrote Mr. Jefferson,
" Find me a gardener
Who can play the french horn?
The bounds of American fortune
Will not admit the indulgence of a domestic band of
Musicians, yet I have thought that a passion for music
Might be reconciled with that economy which we are
Obliged to observe.   I retain among my domestic servants
A gardener, a weaver, a cabinet-maker, and a stone-cutter,
To which I would add a vigneron.   In a country like yours
(id est Burgundy) where music is cultivated and
Practised by every class of men, I suppose there might
Be found persons of these trades who could perform on
The french horn, clarionet, or hautboy and bassoon, so
That one might have a band of two french horns, two
Clarionets, two hautboys and a bassoon, without enlarging
Their domestic expenses.   A certainty of employment for
Half a dozen years
              (*affatigandose per suo piacer o non*)
And at the end of that time, to find them, if they
Choose, a conveyance to their own country, might induce
Them to come here on reasonable wages.   Without meaning to
Give you trouble, perhaps it might be practicable for you

97

In your ordinary intercourse with your people to find out
Such men disposed to come to America. Sobriety and good
Nature would be desirable parts of their characters "
                                        June 1778 Montecello

And in July I went up to Milan for Duke Galeaz
To sponsor his infant in baptism,
Albeit were others more worthy,
And took his wife a gold collar holding a diamond
That cost about 3000 ducats, on which account
That signor Galeaz Sforza Visconti has wished me
To stand sponsor to all of his children.

Another war without glory, and another peace without quiet.

And the Sultan sent him an assassin, his brother;
And the Soldan of Egypt, a lion;
And he begat one pope and one son and four daughters,
And an University, Pisa; (Lauro Medici)
And nearly went broke in his business,
And bought land in Siena and Pisa,
And made peace by his own talk in Naples.
And there was grass on the floor of the temple,
Or where the floor of it might have been;
            Gold fades in the gloom,
                Under the blue-black roof, Placidia's,
Of the exarchate; and we sit here
By the arena, *les gradins*...
And the palazzo, baseless, hangs there in the dawn
With low mist over the tide-mark;·
And floats there nel tramonto
With gold mist over the tide-mark.
The tesserae of the floor, and the patterns.
Fools making new shambles;
                        night over green ocean,
And the dry black of the night.

                    Night of the golden tiger,
And the dry flame in the air,
                    Voices of the procession,
Faint now, from below us,
And the sea with tin flash in the sun-dazzle,
                    Like dark wine in the shadows.
" Wind between the sea and the mountains "
  The tree-spheres half dark against sea
                    half clear against sunset,
The sun's keel freighted with cloud,
And after that hour, dry darkness
Floating flame in the air, gonads in organdy,
Dry flamelet, a petal borne in the wind.
Gignetei kalon.
Impenetrable as the ignorance of old women.
In the dawn, as the fleet coming in after Actium,
Shore to the eastward, and altered,
And the old man sweeping leaves:
        " Damned to you Midas, Midas lacking a Pan! "
And now in the valley,
Valley under the day's edge:
        " Grow with the Pines of Ise;
" As the Nile swells with Inopos.
        " As the Nile falls with Inopos."
Phoibos, turris eburnea,
            ivory against cobalt,
And the boughs cut on the air,
The leaves cut on the air,
The hounds on the green slope by the hill,
        water still black in the shadow.
In the crisp air,
        the discontinuous gods;
Pallas, young owl in the cup of her hand,
And, by night, the stag runs, and the leopard,
Owl-eye amid pine boughs.

Moon on the palm-leaf,
                              confusion;
Confusion, source of renewals;
Yellow wing, pale in the moon shaft,
Green wing, pale in the moon shaft,
Pomegranate, pale in the moon shaft,
White horn, pale in the moon shaft, and Titania
By the drinking hole,
              steps, cut in the basalt.
Danced there Athame, danced, and there Phæthusa
With colour in the vein,
Strong as with blood-drink, once,
With colour in the vein,
Red in the smoke-faint throat.   Dis caught her up.

And the old man went on there
              beating his mule with an asphodel.

XXII

AN' that man sweat blood
to put through that railway,
And what he ever got out of it?
And he said one thing: As it costs,
As in any indian war it costs the government
20,000 dollars per head
To kill off the red warriors, it might be more humane
And even cheaper, to educate.
And there was the other type, Warenhauser,
That beat him, and broke up his business,
Tale of the American Curia that gave him,
Warenhauser permission to build the Northwestern railway
And to take the timber he cut in the process;
So he cut a road through the forest,
Two miles wide, an' perfectly legal.
Who wuz agoin' to stop him!

And he came in and said: Can't do it,
Not at that price, we can't do it."
That was in the last war, here in England,
And he was making chunks for a turbine
In some sort of an army plane;
An' the inspector says: " How many rejects? "
" What you mean, rejects? "
And the inspector says: " How many do you get? "
And Joe said: " We don't get *any* rejects, our..."
And the inspector says: " Well then of course
                                you can't do it."
Price of life in the occident.
And C. H. said to the renowned Mr. Bukos:
" What is the cause of the H. C. L.? " and Mr. Bukos,

The economist consulted of nations, said:

                         "Lack of labour."

And there were two millions of men out of work.
And C. H. shut up, he said
He would save his breath to cool his own porridge,
But I didn't, and I went on plaguing Mr. Bukos
Who said finally: " I am an orthodox
" Economist."

                Jesu Christo!
Standu nel paradiso terrestre
Pensando come si fesse compagna d'Adamo!!

And Mr. H. B. wrote in to the office:
I would like to accept C. H.'s book
But it would make my own seem so out of date.

                Heaven will protect
The lay reader. The whole fortune of
Mac Narpen and Company is founded
Upon Palgrave's Golden Treasury.   Nel paradiso terrestre

And all the material was used up, Jesu Christo,
And everything in its place, and nothing left over
To make una compagna d'Adamo.   Come si fesse?
E poi ha vishtu una volpe
And the tail of the volpe, the vixen,
Fine, spreading and handsome, e pensava:
That will do for this business;
And la volpe saw in his eye what was coming,
Corre, volpe corre, Christu corre, volpecorre,
Christucorre, e dav' un saltu, ed ha preso la coda
Della volpe, and the volpe wrenched loose
And left the tail in his hand, e di questu
Fu fatta,

           e per questu
E la donna una furia,
Una fuRRia-e-una rabbia.

And a voice behind me in the street.
" Meestair Freer!   Meestair..."
And I thought I was three thousand
Miles from the nearest connection;
And he'd known me for three days, years before that,
And he said, one day a week later: Woud you lak
To meet a wholley man, yais he is a veree wholley man.
So I met Mohamed Ben Abt el Hjameed,
And that evening he spent his whole time
Queering the shirt-seller's business,
And taking hot whiskey.   The sailors
Come in there for two nights a week and fill up the café
And the rock scorpions cling to the edge
Until they can't jes' nacherly stand it
And then they go to the Calpe (Lyceo)

NO MEMBER OF THE MILITARY
OF WHATEVER RANK
IS PERMITTED WITHIN THE WALLS
OF THIS CLUB

That fer the governor of Gibel Tara.
" Jeen-jah!   Jeen-jah! " squawked Mohamed,
" O-ah, geef heem sax-pence."
And a chap in a red fez came in, and grinned at Mohamed
Who spat across four metres of tables
At Mustafa.   That was all there was
To that greeting; and three nights later
Ginger came back as a customer, and took it out of Mohamed.
He hadn't sold a damn shirt on the Tuesday.
And I met Yusuf and eight men in the calle,
So I sez: Wot is the matter?
And Yusuf said: Vairy foolish, it will

Be sefen an' seex for the summons
— Mohamed want to sue heem for libel —
To give all that to the court!
             So I went off to Granada
And when I came back I saw Ginger, and I said:
What about it?
             And he said: O-ah, I geef heem a
Seex-pence.   Customs of the sha-ha-reef.
And they were all there in the lyceo,
Cab drivers, and chaps from tobacco shops,
And Edward the Seventh's guide, and they were all
For secession.
Dance halls being closed at two in the morning,
By the governor's order.   And another day on the pier
Was a fat fellah from Rhode Island, a-sayin':
" Bi Hek!   I been all thru Italy
             An' ain't never been stuck! "
" But this place is plumb full er scoundrels."
And Yusuf said: Yais? an' the reech man
In youah countree, haowa they get their money;
They no go rob some poor pairsons?
And the fat fellah shut up, and went off.
And Yusuf said: Woat, he iss all thru Eetaly
An' ee is nevair been stuck, ee ees a liar.
W'en I goa to some forain's country
I am stuck.
             W'en yeou goa to some forain's country
You moss be stuck; w'en they come 'ere I steek thaim.
And we went down to the synagogue,
All full of silver lamps
And the top gallery stacked with old benches;
And in came the levite and six little choir kids
And began yowling the ritual
As if it was crammed full of jokes,
And they went through a whole book of it;

And in came the elders and the scribes
About five or six and the rabbi
And he sat down, and grinned, and pulled out his snuff-box,
And sniffed up a thumb-full, and grinned,
And called over a kid from the choir, and whispered,
And nodded toward one old buffer,
And the kid took him the snuff-box and he grinned,
And bowed his head, and sniffed up a thumb-full,
And the kid took the box back to the rabbi,
And he grinned, e faceva bisbiglio,
And the kid toted off the box to
              another old bunch of whiskers,
And he sniffed up his thumb-full,
And so on till they'd each had his sniff;
And then the rabbi looked at the stranger, and they
All grinned half a yard wider, and the rabbi
Whispered for about two minutes longer,
An' the kid brought the box over to me,
And I grinned and sniffed up my thumb-full.
And then they got out the scrolls of the law
And had their little procession
And kissed the ends of the markers.
And there was a case on for rape and blackmail
Down at the court-house, behind the big patio
              full of wistaria;
An' the nigger in the red fez, Mustafa, on the boat later
An' I said to him: Yusuf, Yusuf's a damn good feller.
And he says:
              " Yais, he ees a goot fello,
" But after all a chew
                            ees a chew."
And the judge says: That veil is too long.
And the girl takes off the veil
That she has stuck onto her hat with a pin,
" Not a veil," she says, " 'at's a scarf."

And the judge says:

       Don't you know you aren't allowed all those buttons?
And she says: Those ain't buttons, them's bobbles.
Can't you see there ain't any button-holes?
And the Judge says: Well, anyway, you're not allowed ermine.
" Ermine? " the girl says, " Not ermine, that ain't,
" 'At's lattittzo."
And the judge says: And just what is a lattittzo?
And the girl says:

       " It'z a animal."

Signori, *you* go and enforce it.

XXIII

ET omniformis," Psellos, " omnis
"Intellectus est." God's fire. Gemisto:
"Never with this religion
"Will you make men of the greeks.
"But build wall across Peloponesus
"And organize, and...
                    damn these Eyetalian barbarians."
And Novvy's ship went down in the tempest
Or at least they chucked the books overboard.

How dissolve Irol in sugar... Houille blanche,
Auto-chenille, destroy all bacteria in the kidney,
Invention-d'entités-plus-ou-moins-abstraits-
en-nombre-égal-aux-choses-à-expliquer...
    La Science ne peut pas y consister. " J'ai
Obtenu une brulure " M. Curie, or some other scientist
"Qui m'a coûté six mois de guérison."
           and continued his experiments.
Tropismes! "We believe the attraction is chemical."

With the sun in a golden cup
    and going toward the low fords of ocean
Ἄλιος δ' Ὑπεριονίδας δέπας ἐσκατέβαινε χρύσεον
Ὄφρα δι ὠκεανοῖο περάσας
    ima vada noctis obscurae
Seeking doubtless the sex in bread-moulds
ἥλιος, ἅλιος, ἄλιος = μάταιος
("Derivation uncertain." The idiot
Odysseus furrowed the sand.)
alixantos, aliotrephès, eiskatebaine, down into,
descended, to the end that, beyond ocean,
pass through, traverse

νυκτὸς ἐρεμνᾶς,   ποτὶ βένθεα
ποτὶ ματέρα, κουριδίαν τ'ἄλοχον
παῖδάς τε φίλους . . . . ἔβα δαφναισι κατάσκιον
Precisely, the selv' oscura
And in the morning, in the Phrygian head-sack
Barefooted, dumping sand from their boat
'Yperionides!
       And the rose grown while I slept,
And the strings shaken with music,
Capriped, the loose twigs under foot;
We here on the hill, with the olives
Where a man might carry his oar up,
And the boat there in the inlet;
As we had lain there in the autumn
Under the arras, or wall painted below like arras,
And above with a garden of rose-trees,
Sound coming up from the cross-street;
As we had stood there,
Watching road from the window,
Fa Han and I at the window,
And her head bound with gold cords.
Cloud over mountain; hill-gap, in mìst, like a sea-coast.

Leaf over leaf, dawn-branch in the sky
And the sea dark, under wind,
The boat's sails hung loose at the mooring,
      Cloud like a sail inverted,
And the men dumping sand by the sea-wall
Olive trees there on the hill
    where a man might carry his oar up.

And my brother De Mænsac
Bet with me for the castle,
And we put it on the toss of a coin,
And I, Austors, won the coin-toss and kept it,

And he went out to Tierci, a jongleur
And on the road for his living,
And twice he went down to Tierci,
And took off the girl there that was just married to Bernart.

And went to Auvergne, to the Dauphin,
And Tierci came with a posse to Auvergnat,
And went back for an army
And came to Auvergne with the army
But never got Pierre nor the woman.
And he went down past Chaise Dieu,
And went after it all to Mount Segur,
    after the end of all things,
And they hadn't left even the stair,
And Simone was dead by that time,
And they called us the Manicheans
Wotever the hellsarse that is.

And that was when Troy was down, all right,
                superbo Ilion...
And they were sailing along
Sitting in the stern-sheets,
Under the lee of an island
And the wind drifting off from the island.
" Tet, tet...
            what is it? " said Anchises.
" Tethnéké," said the helmsman, " I think they
" Are howling because Adonis died virgin."
" Huh! tet..." said Anchises,
            " well, they've made a bloody mess of that city."

" King Otreus, of Phrygia,
" That king is my father."
                and saw then, as of waves taking form,
As the sea, hard, a glitter of crystal,
And the waves rising but formed, holding their form.
No light reaching through them.

XXIV

Tʜᴜs the book of the mandates:

Feb. 1422.

We desire that you our factors give to Zohanne of
Rimini
our servant, six lire marchesini,
for the three prizes he has won racing our barbarisci,
at the rate we have agreed on. The races he has won
are the Modena, the San Petronio at Bologna
and the last race at San Zorzo.

(Signed) Parisina Marchesa

.. pay them for binding
un libro franxese che si chiama Tristano...

Carissimi nostri

Zohanne da Rimini

has won the palio at Milan with our horse and writes that
he is now on the hotel, and wants money.
Send what you think he needs,
but when you get him back in Ferrara find out
what he has done with the first lot, I think over 25 ducats
But send the other cash quickly, as I don't want him
there on the hotel.
... perfumes, parrot seed, combs, two great and two
small ones from Venice, for madama la marxesana...
... 20 ducats to
give to a friend of ours who paid a bill for us
on this trip to Romagna...
... verde colore predeletto, 25 ducats ziparello
silver embroidered for Ugo fiolo del Signore...

(27 nov. 1427)
PROCURATIO NOMINE PATRIS, Leonello Este

(arranging dot for Margarita his sister, to
Roberto Malatesta of Rimini)
natae praelibati margaritae
Ill. D. Nicolai Marchionis Esten. et Sponsae:
The tower of Gualdo
with plenary jurisdiction in civils; and in criminal:
to fine and have scourged all delinquents
as in the rest of their lands,
" which things
this tower, estate at Gualdo had the Illustrious
Nicolaus Marquis of Este received from the said
Don Carlo (Malatesta)
for dower
Illustrae Dominae Parisinae Marxesana."

under my hand D. Michaeli de Magnabucis
Not. pub. Ferr.
D. Nicolaeque Guiduccioli de Arimino.
Sequit bonorum descriptio.

And he in his young youth, in the wake of Odysseus
To Cithera (a. d. 1413) " dove fu Elena rapta da Paris "
Dinners in orange groves, prows attended of dolphins,
Vestige of Rome at Pola, fair wind as far as Naxos
Ora vela, ora a remi, sino ad ora di vespero
Or with the sail tight hauled, by the crook'd land's arm
Zefalonia
And at Corfu, greek singers; by Rhodos
Of the windmills, and to Paphos,
Donkey boys, dust, deserts, Jerusalem, backsheesh
And an endless fuss over passports;
One groat for the Jordan, whether you go there or not,
The school where the madonna in girlhood
Went to learn letters, and Pilate's house closed to the public;
2 soldi for Olivet (to the Saracens)
And no indulgence at Judas's tree; and

" Here Christ put his thumb on a rock
" Saying: hic est medium mundi."
    (That, I assure you, happened.
                        Ego, scriptor cantilenae.)
For worse? for better? but happened.
After which, the greek girls at Corfu, and the
Ladies, Venetian, and they all sang in the evening
Benche niuno cantasse, although none of them could,
Witness Luchino del Campo.
Plus one turkish juggler, and they had a bath
When they got out of Jerusalem
And for cargo: one leopard of Cyprus
And falcons, and small birds of Cyprus,
Sparrow hawks, and grayhounds from Turkey
To breed in Ferrara among thin-legged Ferrarese,
Owls, hawks, fishing tackle.

Was beheaded Aldovrandino (1425, vent'uno Maggio)
Who was cause of this evil, and after
The Marchese asked was Ugo beheaded.   And the Captain:
" Signor... si."   and il Marchese began crying
" Fa me hora tagliar la testa
" dapoi cosi presto hai decapitato il mio Ugo."
Rodendo con denti una bachetta che havea in mani.
And passed that night weeping, and calling Ugo, his son.
Affable, bullnecked, that brought seduction in place of
Rape into government, ter pacis Italiae auctor;
With the boys pulling the tow-ropes on the river
Tre cento bastardi (or bombardi fired off at his funeral)
And the next year a standard from Venice
(Where they'd called off a horse race)
And the baton from the Florentine baily.
" Of Fair aspect, gentle in manner "
Forty years old at the time;
" And they killed a judge's wife among other,

That was a judge of the court and noble,
And called Madonna Laodamia delli Romei,
Beheaded in the pa della justicia;
And in Modena, a madonna Agnesina
Who had poisoned her husband,
" All women known as adulterous,
" That his should not suffer alone."
                    Then the writ ran no further.
And in '31 married Monna Ricarda.

CHARLES... scavoir faisans... et advenir... a haute
noblesse du Linage et Hostel... e faictz hautex...
vaillance... affection... notre dict Cousin...
puissance, auctorite Royal... il et ses hors yssus... et
a leur loise avoir doresenavant
A TOUSIUOURS EN LEURS ARMES ESCARTELURE
... trois fleurs Liz d'or... en champs a'asur dentelle...
ioissent et usent.
                    Mil CCCC trente et ung, conseil
à Chinon, le Roy, l'Esne de la Trimouill,
Vendoise, Jehan Rabateau.

And in '32 came the Marchese Saluzzo
To visit them, his son in law and his daughter,
And to see Hercules his grandson, piccolo e putino.
And in '41 Polenta went up to Venice
Against Niccolo's caution
And was swallowed up in that city.
E fu sepulto nudo, Niccolo,
Without decoration, as ordered in testament,
Ter pacis Italiae.
And if you want to know what became of his statue,
I had a rifle class in Bondeno
And the priest sent a boy to the hardware
And he brought back the nails in a wrapping,

And it was the leaf of a diary
And he got the rest from the hardware
      (Cassini, libraio, speaking)
And on the first leaf of the wrapping
Was how in Napoleon's time
Came down a load of brass fittings from Modena
Via del Po, all went by the river,
To Piacenza for cannon, bells, door-knobs
And the statues of the Marchese Niccolo and of Borso
That were in the Piazza on columns.
And the Commendatore has made it a monograph
Without saying I told him and sent him
The name of the priest.

After him and his day
Were the cake-eaters, the consumers of icing,
That read all day per diletto
And left the night work to the servants;
Ferrara, paradiso dei sarti, " feste stomagose."

" Is it likely Divine Apollo,
That I should have stolen your cattle?
A child of my age, a mere infant,
      And besides, I have been here all night in my crib."
" Albert made me, Tura painted my wall,
And Julia the Countess sold to a tannery...

XXV

THE BOOK OF THE COUNCIL MAJOR
1255 be it enacted:
That they mustn't shoot crap in the hall
of the council, nor in the small court under
pain of 20 danari, be it enacted:
1266 no squire of Venice to throw dice
*any*where in the palace or
in the loggia of the Rialto under pain of ten soldi
or half that for kids, and if they wont pay
they are to be chucked in the water. be it enacted
In libro pactorum
To the things everlasting
memory both for live men and for the future et
quod publice innotescat
in the said date, dicto millessimo
of the illustrious lord, Lord John Soranzo
by god's grace doge of Venice in the Curia
of the Palace of the Doges,
neath the portico next the house of the dwelling of
the Castaldio and of the heralds of the Lord Doge.
being beneath same a penthouse or cages
or room timbered (trabesilis) like a cellar
one Lion male and one female *simul commorantes*
which beasts to the Lord Doge were transmitted small
by that serene Lord King Frederic of Sicily, the
said lion knew carnally and in nature the Lioness
aforesaid and impregnated in that manner that animals
leap on one another to know and impregnate
on the faith of several ocular witnesses
Which lioness bore pregnant for about three months
(as is said by those who saw her assaulted)

and in the said millessimo and month on a sunday
12th. of the month of September about sunrise on
St. Mark's day early but with the light already apparent
the said lioness as is the nature of animals
whelped per naturam three lion cubs vivos et pilosos
living and hairy which born at once began life and motion
and to go gyring about their mother throughout the
aforesaid room as saw the aforesaid Lord Doge and as it
were all the Venetians and other folk who were in
Venice that day that concurred all for this as it were
miraculous sight.   And one of the animals is a male
and the other two female

> I John Marchesini Ducal notary of the
> Venetians as eyewitness saw the
> nativity of these animals thus by
> mandate of the said Doge wrote this
> and put it in file.

Also a note from Pontius Pilate dated the " year 33."

Two columns (a. d. 1323) for the church of St. Nicholas of the
palace 12 lire gross.
To the procurators of St. Marc for entrance to the
palace, for gilding the images and the lion over the door
... to be paid...

Be it enacted:
to Donna Sorantia Soranzo that she come for the
feast of Ascension by night in a covered boat and
alight at the ripa del Palazzo, and when first sees the
Christblood go at once up into the Palace and may
stay in the Palace VIII days to visit the Doge her
father not in that time leaving the palace, nor
descending the palace stair and when she descends it
that she return by night the boat in the like manner

being covered.   To be revoked at the council's pleasure.
                    accepted by 5 of the council

1335. 3 lire 15 groats to stone for making a lion.
1340. Council of the lords noble, Marc Erizio
Nic. Speranzo, Tomasso Gradonico:
                                    that the hall
be new built over the room of the night watch
and over the columns toward the canal where the walk is...

... because of the stink of the dungeons. 1344.
1409... since the most serene Doge can scarce
stand upright in his bedroom...
                        vadit pars, two gross lire
stone stair, 1415, for pulchritude of the palace

                        254 da parte
                            de non 23
                                4 non sincere
Which is to say: they built out over the arches
and the palace hangs there in the dawn, the mist,
in that dimness,
or as one rows in from past the murazzi
the barge slow after moon-rise
and the voice sounding under the sail.
Mist gone.
            And Sulpicia
green shoot now, and the wood
white under new cortex
" as the sculptor sees the form in the air
            before he sets hand to mallet,
" and as he sees the in, and the through,
                            the four sides
" not the one face to the painter
As ivory uncorrupted:
                    " Pone metum Cerinthe "

Lay there, the long soft grass,
                    and the flute lay there by her thigh,
Sulpicia, the fauns, twig-strong,
                              gathered about her;
The fluid, over the grass
Zephyrus, passing through her,
                          " deus nec laedit amantes."
Hic mihi dies sanctus;
And from the stone pits, the heavy voices,
Heavy sound:
                    " Sero, sero...
" Nothing we made, we set nothing in order,
" Neither house nor the carving,
" And what we thought had been thought for too long;
" Our opinion not opinion in evil
" But opinion borne for too long.
" We have gathered a sieve full of water."
And from the comb of reeds, came notes and the chorus
Moving, the young fauns: Pone metum,
Metum, nec deus laedit.

And as after the form, the shadow,
Noble forms, lacking life, that bolge, that valley
the dead words keeping form,
and the cry: Civis Romanus.
The clear air, dark, dark,
The dead concepts, never the solid, the blood rite,
The vanity of Ferrara;

Clearer than shades, in the hill road
Springing in cleft of the rock: Phaethusa
There as she came among them,
Wine in the smoke-faint throat,
Fire gleam under smoke of the mountain,
Even there by meadows of Phlegethon

And against this the flute: pone metum.
Fading, that they carried their guts before them,
And thought then, the deathless,
Form, forms and renewal, gods held in the air,
Forms seen, and then clearness,
Bright void, without image, Napishtim,
Casting his gods back into the *νοῦϛ*.

" as the sculptor sees the form in the air...
" as glass seen under water,
" King Otreus, my father...
and saw the waves taking form as crystal,
notes as facets of air,
and the mind there, before them, moving,
so that notes needed not move.

... side toward the piazza, the worst side of the room
that no one has been willing to tackle,
and do it as cheap or much cheaper...
                    (signed) Tician, 31 May 1513

It being convenient that there be an end to
the painting of Titian, fourth frame from the door on
the right of the hall of the greater council, begun
by maestro Tyciano da Cadore since its being thus
unfinished holds up the decoration of said hall on
the side that everyone sees.   We
move that by authority of this Council maestro Tyciano
aforesaid be constrained to finish said canvas,
and if he have not, to lose the expectancy of the
brokerage on the Fondamenta delli Thodeschi
and moreover to restore all payments recd. on account of
said canvas.   11 Aug. 1522
Ser Leonardus Emo, Sapiens Consilij:
Ser Philippus Capello, Sapiens Terrae Firmae:

119

In 1513 on the last day of May was conceded to
Tician of Cadore painter a succession to a brokerage
on the Fondamenta dei Thodeschi, the first to be vacant
In 1516 on the 5th. of december was declared that
without further waiting a vacancy he shd. enter that
which had been held by the painter Zuan Bellin on
condition that he paint the picture of the land battle
in the Hall of our Greater Council on the side toward
the piazza over the Canal Grande, the which Tician after
the demise of Zuan Bellin entered into possession of the
said Sensaria and has for about twenty years profited by
it, namely to about 100 ducats a year not including the
18 to 20 ducats taxes yearly remitted him it being
fitting that as he has not worked he should not have
the said profits WHEREFORE

                                    be it moved that the said
Tician de Cadore, pictor, be by authority of this Council
obliged and constrained to restore to our government all the
moneys that he has had from the agency during the time he
has not worked on the painting in the said
hall as is reasonable

              ayes 102, noes 38,   37 undecided
                                      register of the senate
                                      terra 1537, carta 136.

XXVI

AND I came here in my young youth
    and lay there under the crocodile
        By the column, looking East on the Friday,
And I said: Tomorrow I will lie on the South side
And the day after, south west.
And at night they sang in the gondolas
And in the barche with lanthorns;
The prows rose silver on silver
        taking light in the darkness. " Relaxetur ! "
11th. December 1461: that Pasti be let out
                    with a caveat
" caveat ire ad Turchum, that he stay out of
                        Constantinople
" if he hold dear our government's pleasure.
" The book will be retained by the council
        (the book being Valturio's " Re Militari ").

To Nicolo Segundino, the next year, 12th. October
" Leave no... omnem... as they say... volve lapidem...
" Stone unturned that he, Pio,
" Give peace to the Malatesta.
" Faithful sons (we are) of the church
            (for two pages)...
" And see all the cardinals and the nephew...
" And in any case get the job done.

" Our galleys were strictly neutral
" And sent there for neutrality.
" See Borso in Ferrara."

121

To Bernard Justinian, 28th. of October:
" Segundino is to come back with the news
" Two or three days after you get this."

Senato Secreto, 28th of October,
Came Messire Hanibal from Cesena :
" Cd. they hoist the flag of St. Mark
" And have Fortinbras and our army? "
" They cd. not... but on the quiet, secretissime,
" Two grand... Sic : He may have
" Two thousand ducats; himself to hire the men
" From our army."
· · · · · · · · ·   · · · · · · · · · ·
... 8 barrels wine, to Henry of Inghilterra...
Tin, serges, amber to go by us to the Levant,
Corfu, and above Corfu...

· ·
And hither came Selvo, doge,
              that first mosiac'd San Marco,
And his wife that would touch food but with forks,
Sed aureis furculis, that is
              with small golden prongs
Bringing in, thus, the vice of luxuria;
And to greet the doge Lorenzo Tiepolo,
Barbers, heads covered with beads,
Furriers, masters in rough,
Master pelters for fine work,
And the masters for lambskin
With silver cups and their wine flasks
And blacksmiths with the gonfaron
              et leurs fioles chargies de vin,
The masters of wool cloth
Glass makers in scarlet
Carrying fabrefactions of glass;

25th April the jousting,
The Lord Nicolo Este,
        Ugaccion dei Contrarini,
The Lord Francesco Gonzaga, and first
The goldsmiths and jewelers' company
Wearing *pellande* of scarlet,
        the horses in cendato —
And it cost three ducats to rent any horse
For three hundred and fifty horses, in piazza,
And the prize was a collar with jewels
And these folk came on horses to the piazza
In the last fight fourteen on a side,
And the prize went to a nigger from Mantua
That came with Messire Gonzaga.

And that year ('38) they came here
Jan. 2.   The Marquis of Ferrara
        mainly to see the greek Emperor,
To take him down the canal to his house,
And with the Emperor came the archbishops:
The Archbishop of Morea Lower
And the Archbishop of Sardis
And the Bishops of Lacedæmon and of Mitylene,
Of Rhodos, of Modon Brandos,
And the Archbishops of Athens, Corinth, and of Trebizond,
The chief secretary and the stonolifex.
And came Cosimo Medici " almost as a Venetian to Venice "
(That would be four days later)
And on the 25th, Lord Sigismundo da Rimini
For government business
And then returned to the camp.
And in February they all packed off
To Ferrara to decide on the holy ghost
And as to the which begat the what in the Trinity. —
Gemisto and the Stonolifex,

And you would have bust your bum laughing
To see the hats and beards of those greeks.

And the guild spirit was declining.
Te fili Dux, tuosque successores
Aureo anulo, to wed the sea as a wife;
for beating the Emperor Manuel,
eleven hundred and seventy six.
1175 a. d. first bridge in Rialto.
" You may seal your acts with lead, Signor Ziani."

The jewelers company had their furs lined with scarlet
And silk cloth for the horses,
A silk cloth called cendato
That they still use for the shawls;
And at the time of that war against Hungary
Uncle Carlo Malatesta, three wounds.
Balista, sword and a lance wound;
And to our general Pandolfo, three legates,
With silk and with silver,
And with velvet, wine and confections, to keep him —
Per animarla — in mood to go on with the fighting.

" That are in San Samuele (young ladies)
            are all to go to Rialto
And to wear yellow kerchief, as are also
Their matrons (ruffiane)."
" Ambassador, for his great wisdom and money,
" That had been here as an exile, Cosimo
" Pater."
" Lord Luigi Gonzaga, to be given Casa Giustinian."

" Bishops of Lampascus and Cyprus
" And other fifty lords bishops
                    that are the church of the orient."

124

March 8, " That Sigismundo left Mantua
Ill contented...

And they are dead and have left a few pictures.
" Albizi have sacked the Medici bank."
" Venetians may stand, come, depart with their families
Free by land, free by sea
                in their galleys,
Ships, boats, and with merchandise.
2% on what's actually sold. No tax above that.
          Year 6962 of the world
            18th. April, in Constantinople."
Wind on the lagoon, the south wind breaking roses.

Illmo ac ex^mo (eccellentissimo) princeps et d^no
Lord, my lord in particular, Sforza:
In reply to 1st l^tr of yr. ld^shp
re mat^r of horses, there are some for sale here.
I said that I hdn't. then seen 'em all thoroughly.
Now I may say that I have, and think
There are eleven good horses and almost that number
Of hacks that might be used in necessity,
To be had at a reasonable price.
It is true that there are X or XI big horses
    from 80 to 110 ducats
That seem to me dearer at the price
Than those for 80 ducats and under
And I think that if yr. ld^sp wd. send from
1000 ducats to one thousand 500 it cd. be spent
On stuff that wd. suit yr. L^dp quite well.
Please Y. L. to answer quickly
As I want to take myself out of here,
And if you want me to buy them
Send the cash by Mr. Pitro the farrier
And have him tell me by mouth or letter

What yr. ld^p wants me to buy.
Even from 80 ducats up there are certain good horses.
I have nothing else to say to your Lordship
Save my salutations.
Given Bologna, 14th. of August 1453
    Servant of yr. Illustrious Lordship
               PISANELLUS

1462, 12th December: " and Vittor Capello
Brought also the head of St. George the Martyr
From the Island of Siesina.
This head was covered with silver and
Taken to San Giorgio Maggiore.

To the Cardinal Gonzaga of Mantua, ultimo febbraio 1548
" 26th of feb. was killed in this city
Lorenzo de Medicis. Yr. Illu^s L^dshp will understand
from the enc. account how the affair is said to have
gone off. They say those who killed him have certainly
got away in a post boat with 6 oars. But they don't
know which way they have gone, and as a guard may
have been set in certain places and passes, it wd.
be convenient if yr. Ill^s L^dshp wd. write at once
to your ambassador here, saying among other things
that the two men who killed Lorenzino have passed through
the city of Mantua and that no one knows which
way they have gone. Publishing this information
from yr. Ldshp will perhaps help them to get free.
Although we think they are already in Florence, but
in any case this measure can do no harm. So that
yr. Ldshp wd. benefit by doing it quickly and even
to have others send the same news.
May Our Lord protect yr. Ill^s and most Rev^nd person
with the increase of state you desire.
               Venice, last of Feb. 1548
               I kiss the hands of yr. Ill. Ld^shp
               Don In. Hnr. de Mendoça

To the Marquis of Mantova, Fran° Gonzaga
Illustrious my Lord, during the past few days
An unknown man was brought to me by some others
To see a Jerusalem I have made, and as soon as he
saw it he insisted that I sell it him, saying it
gave him the gtst. content and satisfac^{tn}
Finally the deal was made and he took it away,
without paying and hasn't since then appeared.
I went to tell the people who had brought him, one
of whom is a priest with a beard that wears a
grey berettino whom I have often seen with you in
the hall of the gtr. council and I asked him the
fellow's name, and it is a Messire Lorenzo, the
painter to your Lordship, from which I have easily
understood what he was up to, and on that account
I am writing you, to furnish you my name and the
work's.   In the first place illustrious m. lord, I am
that painter to the Seignory, commissioned to paint the
gt. hall where Yr. Lordship deigns to mount
on the scaffold to see our work, the history of Ancona,
and my name is Victor Carpatio.
As to the Jerusalem I dare say there is not another
in our time as good and completely perfect, or as
large.   It is 25 ft. long by 5 1/2, and I know Zuane
Zamberti has often spoken of it to yr.   Sublimity; I
know certainly that this painter of yours has carried
off a piece, not the whole of it.   I can send you
a small sketch in aquarelle on a roll, or have it
seen by good judges and leave the price to your
Lordship.
XV.   Aug 1511, Venetijs.

                         I have sent a copy of
this letter by another way to be sure you get one or the other.
       The humble svt. of yr. Sublimity
                            Victor Carpathio
                               pictore.

To the supreme pig, the archbishop of Salzburg:
Lasting filth and perdition.
Since your exalted pustulence is too stingy
To give me a decent income
And has already assured me that here I have nothing to hope
And had better seek fortune elsewhere;
And since thereafter you have
Three times impeded my father and self intending departure
I ask you for the fourth time
To behave with more decency, and this time
Permit my departure.

Wolfgang Amadeus, august 1777
(inter lineas)

" As is the sonata, so is little Miss Cannabich."

XXVII

FORMANDO di disio nuova persona
    One man is dead, and another has rotted his end off
    Et quant au troisième
    Il est tombé dans le
De sa femme, on ne le reverra
Pas, oth fugol ouitbaer:
" Observed that the paint was
Three quarters of an inch thick and concluded,
As they were being rammed through, the age of that
Cruiser." " Referred to no longer as
The goddamned Porta-goose, but as
England's oldest ally." " At rests in calm zone
If possible, the men are to be fed and relaxed,
The officers on the contrary..."
Ten million germs in his face,
" That is part of the risk and happens
" About twice a year in tubercular research, Dr. Spahlinger..."
" J'ai obtenu " said M. Curie, or some other scientist
" A burn that cost me six months in curing,"
And continued his experiments.
England off there in black darkness,
Russia off there in black darkness,
The last crumbs of civilization...
And they elected a Prince des Penseurs
Because there were so damn many princes,
And they elected a Monsieur Brisset
Who held that man is descended from frogs;
And there was a cracked concierge that they
Nearly got into the Deputies,
To protest against the earthquake in Messina.
    The Bucentoro sang it in that year,

1908, 1909, 1910, and there was
An old washerwoman beating her washboard,
That would be 1920, with a cracked voice,
Singing " Stretti! " and that was the last
Till this year, '27, Hotel Angioli, in Milan,
With an air Clara d'Ellébeuse,
With their lakelike and foxlike eyes,
With an air " Benette joue la Valse des Elfes "
In the salotto of that drummer's hotel,
Two young ladies with their air de province:
" No, we are Croat merchants, commercianti,
" There is nothing strange in our history."
" No, not to sell, but to buy."

And there was that music publisher,
The fellow that brought back the shrunk Indian head
Boned, oiled, from Bolivia, said:
" Yes, I went out there. Couldn't make out the trade,
Long after we'd melt up the plates,
Get an order, 200 copies, Peru,
Or some station in Chile."
Took out Floradora in sheets,
And brought back a red-headed mummy.
With an air Clara d'Ellébeuse, singing " Stretti."

Sed et universus quoque ecclesie populus,
All rushed out and built the duomo,
Went as one man without leaders
And the perfect measure took form;
" Glielmo ciptadin " says the stone, " the author,
" And Nicolao was the carver "
Whatever the meaning may be.
And they wrote for year after year.
Refining the criterion,
Or they rose as the tops subsided;

Brumaire, Fructidor, Petrograd.
And Tovarisch lay in the wind
And the sun lay over the wind,
And three forms became in the air
And hovered about him,
                  so that he said:
This machinery is very ancient,
                  surely we have heard this before.
And the waves like a forest
Where the wind is weightless in the leaves
But moving,
          so that the sound runs upon sound.
          Xarites, born of Venus and wine.

Carved stone upon stone.
But in sleep, in the waking dream,
Petal'd the air;
          twig where but wind-streak had been;
Moving bough without root,
                  by Helios.
So that the Xarites bent over tovarisch.
And these are the labours of tovarisch,
That tovarisch lay in the earth,
And rose, and wrecked the house of the tyrants,
And that tovarisch then lay in the earth
          And the Xarites bent over tovarisch.

These are the labours of tovarisch,
That tovarisch wrecked the house of the tyrants,
And rose, and talked folly on folly,
And walked forth and lay in the earth
          And the Xarites bent over tovarisch.

And that tovarisch cursed and blessed without aim,
          These are the labours of tovarisch,

Saying:
> "Me Cadmus sowed in the earth
> And with the thirtieth autumn
I return to the earth that made me.
Let the five last build the wall;

I neither build nor reap.
That he came with the gold ships, Cadmus,
That he fought with the wisdom,
Cadmus, of the gilded prows. Nothing I build
And I reap
Nothing; with the thirtieth autumn
I sleep, I sleep not, I rot
And I build no wall.
> Where was the wall of Eblis
At Ventadour, there now are the bees,
And in that court, wild grass for their pleasure
That they carry back to the crevice
Where loose stone hangs upon stone.
I sailed never with Cadmus,
> lifted never stone above stone."

" Baked and eaten tovarisch!
" Baked and eaten, tovarisch, my boy,
" That is your story. And up again,
" Up and at 'em. Laid never stone upon stone."

" The air burst into leaf."
" Hung there flowered acanthus,
" Can you tell the down from the up? "

XXVIII

AND God the Father Eternal (Boja d'un Dio!)
Having made all things he cd.
think of, felt yet
That something was lacking, and thought
Still more, and reflected that
The Romagnolo was lacking, and
Stamped with his foot in the mud and
Up comes the Romagnolo:
"Gard, yeh bloudy 'angman! It's me".
Aso iqua me. All Esimo Dottor Aldo Walluschnig
Who with the force of his intellect
With art and assiduous care
Has snatched from death by a most perilous operation
The classical Caesarean cut
Marotti, Virginia, in Senni of San Giorgio
At the same time saving her son.
May there move to his laud the applause of all men
And the gratitude of the family.
S. Giorgio, 23d May. A.D. 1925.
Item: There are people that can swimme in the sea
Havens and rivers naked
Having bowes and shafts,
Coveting to draw nigh yr. shippe which if they find not
Well watched and warded they wil assault
Desirous of the bodies of men which they covet for meate,
If you resist them
They dive and wil flee.
And Mr Lourpee sat on the floor of the pension dining-room
Or perhaps it was in the alcove
And about him lay a great mass of pastells,
That is, stubs and broken pencils of pastell,

In pale indeterminate colours.
And he admired the Sage of Concord
        " Too broad ever to make up his mind ".
And the mind of Lourpee at fifty
Directed him into a room with a certain vagueness
As if he wd.
neither come in nor stay out
As if he wd.
go neither to the left nor the right
And his painting reflected this habit.
And Mrs Kreffle's mind was made up,
Perhaps by the pressure of circumstance,
She described her splendid apartment
In Paris and left without paying her bill
And in fact she wrote later from Sevilla
And requested a shawl, and received it
From the Senora at 300 pesetas cost to the latter
(Also without remitting) which
May have explained the lassitude of her daughter;
And the best paid dramatic critic
Arrived from Manhattan
And was lodged in a bordello (promptly)
Having trusted " his people "
Who trusted a Dutch correspondent,
And when they had been devoured by fleas
(Critic and family)
They endeavoured to break the dutchman's month's contract,
And the ladies from West Virginia
Preserved the natal aroma,
And in the railway feeding-room in Chiasso
She sat as if waiting for the train for Topeka
— That was the year of the strikes —
When we came up toward Chiasso
By the last on the narrow-gauge,
Then by tramway from Como

Leaving the lady who loved bullfights
With her eight trunks and her captured hidalgo,
And a dutchman was there who was going
To take the boat at Trieste,
Sure, he was going to take it;
Would he go round by Vienna? He would not.
Absence of trains wdnt. stop him.
So we left him at last in Chiasso
Along with the old woman from Kansas,
Solid Kansas, her daughter had married that Swiss
Who kept the buffet in Chiasso.
Did it shake her? It did not shake her.
She sat there in the waiting room, solid Kansas,
Stiff as a cigar-store indian from the Bowery
Such as one saw in " the nineties ",
First sod of bleeding Kansas
That had produced this ligneous solidness;
If thou wilt go to Chiasso wilt find that indestructable female
As if waiting for the train to Topeka
In the buffet of that station on the bench that
Follows the wall, to the right side as you enter.
And Clara Leonora wd. come puffing so that one
Cd. hear her when she reached the foot of the stairs,
Squared, chunky, with her crooked steel spectacles
And her splutter and her face full of teeth
And old Rennert wd. sigh heavily
And look over the top of his lenses and
She wd. arrive after due interval with a pinwheel
Concerning Grillparzer or — pratzer
Or whatever follow the Grill —, and il Gran Maestro
Mr Liszt had come to the home of her parents
And taken her on his prevalent knee and
She held that a sonnet was a sonnet
And ought never be destroyed,
And had taken a number of courses

135

And continued with hope of degrees and
Ended in a Baptist learnery
        Somewhere near the Rio Grande.

And they wanted more from their women,
Wanted 'em jacked up a little
And sent over for teachers (Ceylon)
So Loica went out and died there
After her time in the post-Ibsen movement.

And one day in Smith's room
Or may be it was that 1908 medico's
Put the gob in the fire-place
Ole Byers and Feigenbaum and Joe Bromley,
Joe hittin' the gob at 25 feet
Every time, ping on the metal
        (Az ole man Comley wd. say: Boys!...
        Never cherr terbakker! Hrwwkke tth!
        Never cherr terbakker!,
" Missionaries," said Joe, " I was out back of Jaffa,
I dressed in the costume, used to like the cafés,
All of us settin' there on the ground,
Pokes his head in the doorway: " Iz there any,"
He says, " Gar'
Damn
Man here
Thet kan speak ENGLISH? "
        Nobody said anything fer a while
And then I said: " Hu er' you? "
" I'm er misshernary I am "
He sez, " chucked off a naval boat in Shanghaï.
I worked at it three months, nothin' to live on."
Beat his way overland.
I never saw the twenty I lent him."

Great moral secret service, plan, Tribune is told
limit number to thirty thousand,

only highest type will be included,
propaganda within ranks of the veterans,
to keep within bounds when they come into
contact with personal liberty...with the french authorities...
that includes the Paris police...
Strengthen franco-american amity.

NARCOTIC CHARGE: Frank Robert Iriquois
gave his home Oklahoma City... Expelled July 24 th.

" Je suis...
(Across the bare planks of a diningroom in the Pyrenees)
   ... plus fort que...
      ... le Boud-hah! "
(No contradiction)
" Je suis...
   ... plus fort que le...
      ... Christ!
(No contradiction)
" J'aurais...
   aboli...
    le poids! "
(Silence, somewhat unconvinced.)
And in his waste house, detritus,
As it were the cast buttons of splendours,
The harbour of Martinique, drawn every house, and in detail.
Green shutters on half the houses,
Half the thing still unpainted.
       "... sont
" l'in.. fan... terie кон-
    lon-
     i-ale "
voce tinnula
" Ce sont les vieux Marsouins! "
He made it, feitz Marcebrus, the words and the music,

137

Uniform out for Peace Day
And that lie about the Tibetan temple
(happens by the way to be true,
they do carry you up on their shoulders) but
Bad for his medical practice.
" Retreat? " said Dr Wymans, " It was marrvelous...
Gallipoli...
Secret.   Turks knew nothing about it.
Uh! Helped me to get my wounded aboard."
And that man sweat blood to put through that railway,
And what he ever got out of it?
And one day he drove down to the whorehouse
Cause all the farmers had consented
                and granted the right of way,
But the pornoboskos wdn't. have it at any price
And said he'd shoot the surveyors,
But he didn't shoot ole pop in the buckboard,
He giv him the right of way.
And they thought they had him flummox'd,
Nobody'd sell any rails;
Till he went up to the north of New York state
And found some there on the ground
And he had 'em pried loose and shipped 'em
And had 'em laid here through the forest.

Thing is to find something simple
As for example Pa Stadtvolk;
Hooks to hang gutters on roofs,
A spike and half-circle, patented 'em and then made 'em;
Worth a good million, not a book in the place;
Got a horse about twenty years after, seen him
                Of a Saturday afternoon
When they'd taken down an old fence,
Ole Pa out there knockin the nails out
(To *save* 'em). I hear he smoked good cigars.

And when the Prince Oltrepassimo died, saccone,
That follow the coffins,
He lay there on the floor of the chapel
On a great piece of patterned brocade
And the walls solid gold about him
And there was a hole in one of his socks
And the place open that day to the public,
Kids running in from the street
And a cat sat there licking himself
And then stepped over the Principe,
Discobolus upstairs and the main door
Not opened since '70
When the Pope shut himself into the Vatican
And they had scales on the table
To weigh out the food on fast days;
And he lay there with his hood back
And the hole in one of his socks.

" Buk! " said the Second Baronet, " eh...
" Thass a funny lookin' buk " said the Baronet
Looking at Bayle, folio, 4 vols. in gilt leather, " Ah...
" Wu... Wu... wot you goin' eh to do with ah...
" ... ah read-it? "
                    Sic loquitur eques.

And lest it pass with the day's news
Thrown out with the daily paper,
Neither official pet
Nor Levine with the lucky button
Went on into darkness,
Saw naught above but close dark,
Weight of ice on the fuselage
Borne into the tempest, black cloud wrapping their wings,
The night hollow beneath them
And fell with dawn into ocean

But for the night saw neither sky nor ocean
And found ship... why?... how?... by the Azores.
And she was a bathing beauty, Miss Arkansas or Texas
And the man (of course) quasi anonymous
Neither a placard for non-smokers or non-alcohol
Nor for the code of Peoria;'
Or one-eyed Hinchcliffe and Elsie
Blackeyed bitch that married dear Dennis,
That flew out into nothingness
And her father was the son of one too
That got the annulment.

XXIX

PEARL, great sphere, and hollow,
    Mist over lake, full of sunlight,
    Pernella concubina
    The sleeve green and shot gold over her hand
Wishing her son to inherit
Expecting the heir ainé be killed in battle
He being courageous, poisoned his brother puiné
Laying blame on Siena
And this she did by a page
Bringing war once more on Pitigliano
And the page repented and told this
To Nicolo (ainé) Pitigliano
Who won back that rock from his father
" still doting on Pernella his concubine ".
        The sand that night like a seal's back
        Glossy beneath the lanthorns.
From the Via Sacra
        (fleeing what band of Tritons)
Up to the open air
Over that mound of the hippodrome:
Liberans et vinculo ab omni liberatos
As who with four hands at the cross roads
By king's hand or sacerdos'
        are given their freedom
— Save who were at Castra San Zeno...

Cunizza for God's love, for remitting the soul of her father
— May hell take the traitors of Zeno.
And fifth begat he Alberic
And sixth the Lady Cunizza.

In the house of the Cavalcanti

Free go they all as by full manumission
All serfs of Eccelin my father da Romano
Save those who were with Alberic at Castra San Zeno
And let them go also
The devils of hell in their body.

And sixth the Lady Cunizza
That was first given Richard St Boniface
And Sordello subtracted her from that husband
And lay with her in Tarviso
Till he was driven out of Tarviso
And she left with a soldier named Bonius
nimium amorata in eum
And went from one place to another
" The light of this star o'ercame me "
Greatly enjoying herself
And running up the most awful bills.
And this Bonius was killed on a sunday
and she had then a Lord from Braganza
and later a house in Verona.

And he looked from the planks to heaven,
Said Juventus: " Immortal...
He said: " Ten thousand years before now...
Or he said: " Passing into the point of the cone
You begin by making the replica.
Thus Lusty Juventus, in September,
In cool air, under sky,
Before the residence of the funeral director
Whose daughters' conduct caused comment.
But the old man did not know how he felt
Nor cd. remember what prompted the utterance.
He said: " What I know, I have known,
" How can the knowing cease knowing? "

By the lawn of the senior elder
He continued his ambulation:
" Matter is the lightest of all things,
" Chaff, rolled into balls, tossed, whirled in the aether,
" Undoubtedly crushed by the weight,
" Light also proceeds from the eye;
" In the globe over my head
" Twenty feet in diameter, thirty feet in diameter
" Glassy, the glaring surface —
" There are many reflections
" So that one may watch them turning and moving
" With heads down now, and now up.
He went on toward the amateur student of minerals
That later went bankrupt;
He went on past the house of the local funny man,
Jo Tyson that had a camera. His daughter was bow-legged
And married the assembly-man's son.

              O-hon dit que-ke fois au vi'-a-ge...

Past the house of the three retired clergymen
Who were too cultured to keep their jobs.
Languor has cried unto languor
            about the marshmallow-roast
(Let us speak of the osmosis of persons)
The wail of the phonograph has penetrated their marrow
(Let us...
The wail of the pornograph....)
        The cicadas continue uninterrupted.
With a vain emptiness the virgins return to their homes
With a vain exasperation
The ephèbe has gone back to his dwelling,
The djassban has hammered and hammered,
The gentleman of fifty has reflected
            That it is perhaps just as well.
Let things remain as they are.

The mythological exterior lies on the moss in the forest
And questions him about Darwin.
And with a burning fire of phantasy
                    he replies with "Deh! nuvoletta..."
So that she would regret his departure.
                    Drift of weed in the bay:
She seeking a guide, a mentor,
He aspires to a career with honour
To step in the tracks of his elders;
                    a greater incomprehension?
There is no greater incomprehension
Than between the young and the young.
The young seek comprehension;
The middleaged to fulfill their desire.
Sea weed dried now, and now floated,
                    mind drifts, weed, slow youth, drifts,
Stretched on the rock, bleached and now floated;
Wein, Weib, TAN AOIDAN
Chiefest of these the second, the female
Is an element, the female
Is a chaos
An octopus
A biological process
                    and we seek to fulfill...
TAN AOIDAN, our desire, drift...
                    Ailas e que'm fau miey huelh
                    Quar no vezon so qu'ieu vuelh.
Our mulberry leaf, woman, TAN AOIDAN,
" Nel ventre tuo, o nella mente mia,
" Yes, Milady, precisely, if you wd.
have anything properly made."

" Faziamo tutte le due...
" No, not in the palm-room ".   The lady says it is
Too cold in the palm-room.   Des valeurs,

144

Nom de Dieu, et
     encore des valeurs.

She is submarine, she is an octopus, she is
A biological process,
So Arnaut turned there
Above him the wave pattern cut in the stone
Spire-top alevel the well-curb
And the tower with cut stone above that, saying:
     " I am afraid of the life after death."
and after a pause:
" Now, at last, I have shocked him."
And another day or evening toward sundown by the arena
(les gradins)
A little lace at the wrist
And not very clean lace either...
And I, " But this beats me,
" Beats me, I mean that I do not understand it;
" This love of death that is in them."
          Let us consider the osmosis of persons
nondum orto jubare;
The tower, ivory, the clear sky
Ivory rigid in sunlight
And the pale clear of the heaven
Phoibos of narrow thighs,
The cut cool of the air,
Blossom cut on the wind, by Helios
Lord of the Light's edge, and April
Blown round the feet of the God,
Beauty on an ass-cart
Sitting on five sacks of laundry
That wd. have been the road by Perugia
That leads out to San Piero. Eyes brown topaz,
Brookwater over brown sand,
The white hounds on the slope,

Glide of water, lights and the prore,
Silver beaks out of night,
Stone, bough over bough,
      lamps fluid in water,
Pine by the black trunk of its shadow
And on hill black trunks of the shadow
The trees melted in air.

XXX

OMPLEYNT, compleynt I hearde upon a day,
   Artemis singing, Artemis, Artemis
   Agaynst Pity lifted her wail:
   Pity causeth the forests to fail,
Pity slayeth my nymphs,
Pity spareth so many an evil thing.
Pity befouleth April,
Pity is the root and the spring.
Now if no fayre creature followeth me
It is on account of Pity,
It is on account that Pity forbideth them slaye.
All things are made foul in this season,
This is the reason, none may seek purity
Having for foulnesse pity
And things growne awry;
No more do my shaftes fly
To slay.   Nothing is now clean slayne
But rotteth away.

In Paphos, on a day
                I also heard:
... goeth not with young Mars to playe
But she hath pity on a doddering fool,
She tendeth his fyre,
She keepeth his embers warm.

Time is the evil. Evil.
                A day, and a day
Walked the young Pedro baffled,
                a day and a day

After Ignez was murdered.

Came the Lords in Lisboa
                              a day, and a day
In homage. Seated there
                              dead eyes,
Dead hair under the crown,
The King still young there beside her.

Came Madame ῩΛΗ
Clothed with the light of the altar
And with the price of the candles.
"Honour? Balls for yr. honour!
Take two million and swallow it."
                              Is come Messire Alfonso
And is departed by boat for Ferrara
And has passed here without saying " O."

Whence have we carved it in metal
Here working in Caesar's fane:
                  To the Prince Caesare Borgia
                  Duke of Valent and Aemelia
...and here have I brought cutters of letters
and printers not vile and vulgar
                  (in Fano Caesaris)
notable and sufficient compositors
and a die-cutter for greek fonts and hebrew
named Messire Francesco da Bologna
not only of the usual types but he hath excogitated
a new form called cursive or chancellry letters
nor was it Aldous nor any other but it was
this Messire Francesco who hath cut all Aldous his letters
with such grace and charm as is known
                  Hieronymous Soncinus 7th July 1503.
and as for text we have taken it

148

from that of Messire Laurentius
and from a codex once of the Lords Malatesta...

And in August that year died Pope Alessandro Borgia,
Il Papa mori.

Explicit canto
XXX

New Directions Paperbooks—A Partial Listing

For complete listing request free catalog from
New Directions, 80 Eighth Avenue, New York 10011   †Bilingual

**For complete listing request free catalog from
New Directions, 80 Eighth Avenue, New York 10011**

†Bilingual